UNIVERSITY OF NORTH CAROLINA
STUDIES IN COMPARATIVE LITERATURE

NUMBER 36

# UNIVERSITY OF NORTH CAROLINA
## STUDIES IN COMPARATIVE LITERATURE

*Editorial Committee*

Foreign Sales through Librairie E. Droz, 8 Rue Verdaine, Geneva, Switzerland.

# FLUMEN HISTORICUM
# VICTOR COUSIN'S AESTHETIC
# AND ITS SOURCES

BY

FREDERIC WILL

CHAPEL HILL
THE UNIVERSITY OF NORTH CAROLINA PRESS
1965

B
2268
A3W5

*Printed in the Netherlands by Royal VanGorcum Ltd., Assen*

*For my father*

# *Preface*

This study is related to two previous works: to my doctoral dissertation, submitted to Yale University in 1954, and to a later book, *Intelligible Beauty in Aesthetic Thought* (Tübingen, 1957). The present argument is, in a sense, a rewriting and rethinking of part of the dissertation, the part which centers on the sources of Cousin's aesthetic. *Intelligible Beauty in Aesthetic Thought* also addressed itself to this problem, though more peripherally than the thesis did. There are substantial areas of overlapping, between this study and the dissertation. Between this study and the book there is overlapping at one point; where the book treats Plato and Plotinus. (Parts of pages 19-31 of the book). I have permitted this overlapping to stay as it is. I was unable to put the historical points more satisfactorily than I had done earlier. With this exception, which I think hardly an exception, the present work is independent. It is a unique study of Cousin's aesthetic, and of its sources and importance. It is exclusively an essay in comparative aesthetics, and it returns all its comparisons to *a single point;* Victor Cousin's thought.

For the help which has enabled me to bring these matters to publication, I am greatly appreciative. Professor René Wellek, of Yale, gave the first pushes, opening my mind – to change metaphors – to issues and personages which had been quite foreign to me. At the same time, during that apprenticeship at Yale, Professors Henri Peyre and W. K. Wimsatt were teaching me. They served, along with Professor Wellek, as the completing members in a trinity of most instructive influences. My gratitude to these men grows annually.

There would be no point in trying to acknowledge the rest of the help: it is too various and too valuable to be catalogued impersonally. It will be enough, I think, to put down three additional salient debts: to the University of Iowa Graduate College, for financial help; to Professor Werner Friederich, who has for some years, though hardly knowing me, cheerfully and effectually helped my efforts to find a professional career teaching comparative literature; and to my wife, qui comprend mieux que moi.

*Iowa City, Iowa*
*January, 1965.*

# Contents

# I

Victor Cousin was not a great philosopher, as is clear from any of his philosophical writings. His language was rhetorical, his thought often naively and pompously idealistic, and his general attitude overbearing. To be sure, his lectures and writings played a large role in the formation of the Romantic temperament in France; but that was partly because of the post-revolutionary drought of ideas, and partly because of the impoverishment of French philosophy at the time.

I am not interested, however, in writing a general critique of Cousin. That would not be original. Jules Simon and Paul Janet have already devoted general evaluative books to the matter. Janet's is an especially sound and generous evaluation of Cousin. What I want to do is different. It is to discuss Cousin's aesthetic and its sources, while at the same time considering the question of what it all means.

The often dull job of source-searching proves exciting in this case.

Before it can begin, before even a short exposition of Cousin's aesthetic can be given, I must say a word about two key aspects of his general philosophy: his Eclecticism, and his theory of knowledge.

Cousin is known as the founder of the philosophical school of Eclecticism, which reigned in early 19th century France, and which succeeded the Idéologisme of Destutt de Tracy, Cabanis,

1

and others. This is the language of philosophy text-books. What did Eclecticism mean? Cousin's program was to

> dégager ce qu'il y a de vrai en chacun de ces systèmes (previous philosophical systems) et en composer une philosophie supérieure à tous les systèmes qui les gouverne tous en les dominant tous.[1]

This was the opening cry of his philosophy: he launched it in 1818, in the first edition *Du Vrai, Du Beau, et Du Bien*, his chief philosophical work. Yet what it involved, in his practice, was not a new way of approaching the history of philosophy, or even of approaching the creation of it: it was a new interest in the history of philosophy. As a method for interpreting that history the formula was useless, because it implied that the truth in the thought of the past could be torn cleanly away from the untruth. But as a statement of faith in the importance of historical-philosophical thought Cousin's Eclecticism was significant.

Such an eclectic method needs to rest on principles by which truth and falsity can be recognized and separated. But Cousin was not careful to harmonize – that is to adjust – his principles to his approach to history. The impression is often left that his Eclecticism and his own philosophy are two quite separate things. I will say another word about this shortly.

Cousin's theory of knowledge is the kernel of his own philosophy. In it his chief struggle was to repudiate the implications of Kant's first *Kritik*, whether they are found in history or in creative philosophical thought. For this fight Cousin elaborated a 'théorie de la raison' by which he claimed that man could attain ultimate valid knowledge of reality. 'Raison,' he said, is an impersonal power, native to every human, which provides spontaneous knowledge of absolute truth.

> Elle (la raison) tombe sous l'observation aussi bien que la sensibilité et la liberté. C'est dans cette sphère que l'observation saisit immédiatement des principes qui, aussitôt qu'ils apparaissent à l'observation, lui apparaissent intérieurs, postérieurs, supérieurs à elle-même, indépendants d'elle-même, vrais en tout temps et en

2

tout lieu, parce qu'ils sont vrais en eux-mêmes, c'est à dire, vrais d'une vérité absolue.[2]

'Raison' is observed, or realized, through 'abstraction immédiate.' By this act – possible to all men – an object of cognition is stripped of its contingent, particular elements, and becomes an unmediated knowledge of truth. In working on a mathematical or historical problem I suddenly find the particulars of the problem yielding to their absolute truth: a truth which certifies itself as independent of me. Cousin tries hard to defend this conception but he is unsuccessful. His failure in defense, at this strategic point, is a great weakness.

These theories, of 'raison' and of 'abstraction immédiate,' play some part in Cousin's writing of the history of philosophy: a qualification of the impression that his Eclecticism and his own thought are quite separate. He wrote much about the history of philosophy, and his critiques of Locke, Hume, and Reid are still worth reading. The main argument there is that Locke's theory of knowledge brought on a crisis in eighteenth century philosophy. Locke mistakenly – Cousin says – claimed that the content of the mind may have its origin entirely in sensation; a sort of reductionism of ideas. Hume's extreme and dangerous skepticism is only the logical conclusion from Locke: a suspicion toward the validity and reality of ideas. Reid thought, in an exemplary way, that ideas and sensation, the spiritual and material world, are both equally existent and valid and that our ideas are adjusted to things as they are. Cousin admired this position. His own theories are plainly the source of these judgments.

But all that this proves, I think, is that Cousin's own thought and his history of thought are related. There is a normal, inter-critical relation between them. Nowhere has Cousin contributed, through his Eclecticism, any novel method or attitude toward the history of philosophy. There is a break in what might have been the deep continuity of Cousin's thought: the continuity between his creative thought and his relation to history.

3

# II

Cousin's first writing on aesthetic appeared in an article called 'Du Beau Réel et du Beau Idéal,' which was published in 1816, in *Premiers Essais de Philosophie*, and again in his *Fragments Philosophiques* in 1826: he argues for a neoclassical 'ideal' model of beauty, by which an artist creates, and an observer judges, beauty. This 'ideal,' he held, is in the mind, and is co-experienced with the real beauty of the object. 'Real' beauty has two elements: an individual, contingent element; and an essential, unchanging element. These elements are co-experienced by two corresponding 'faculties' of the mind, 'raison,' and 'amour,' the first directed to the unchangeable or general element of the object, the second to the contingent element. This conception of 'ideal beauty,' which is superimposed on a twofold 'real' beauty, which itself contains an essential element, is obtained by an 'abstraction immédiate' of the kind involved in a realization of 'raison.'

The substance of this early essay enters in decreasing importance into Cousin's editions of *Du Vrai, Du Beau, et Du Bien*. In the 1836 edition, based on notes taken in Cousin's original class of 1818, and the only edition not retouched by him later, the twenty-first lesson reproduces essentially this early essay. But there is also to be found a doctrine of moral beauty, which exists wholly on the level of the 'beau réel.' Here I want only to

4

remark that this 'doctrine' makes it possible, on the level of 'real beauty,' to attain the heights of aesthetic experience, to approach God, the absolute spirit. I shall point out that Cousin never fuses his 'beau idéal' *artistic* concept with the theory of ascension through *moral* beauty, which he inherits from the Platonic tradition.

The conspicuous change in Cousin's aesthetic appears in the 1853 edition of *Du Vrai, Du Beau, et Du Bien*. There he says nothing of his 'théorie de la raison' as applied to beauty. He tends to fuse the neoclassic and Platonic conceptions by making God, the supreme beauty, the 'terme' both of ascension through moral beauty, and of the 'beau idéal.' He writes:

> Dieu étant le principe de toutes choses doit être à ce titre celui de la beauté parfaite, et *par conséquent* de toutes les beautés naturelles qui l'expriment plus ou moins imparfaitement.... (my under-linings.)[3]

As it evolves toward a vague spiritualism, Cousin's aesthetic moves from a confusingly complex intellectual solution to a confusingly vague solution. The first solution is more helpful here, in the attempt to understand his specifically 'aesthetic' ideas, and I shall work mainly with the 1836 edition of *Du Vrai* – with such ideas as Lesson twenty-one presents – unless I indicate otherwise.[4]

In all aesthetic thinking Cousin sets himself an idealistic goal, while limiting, toward 1853, the technical demonstrations. For him, beauty is always the object of intelligible experience, as are truth and goodness. The first requirement of a science of beauty, he believes, is a systematic structure, since only so can the relationships of beauty to other facets of experiences be understood. If the mere 'feeling' of beauty is followed where it leads, no real conception of the nature of beauty is possible.[5] And even if it is understood confusedly, the ultimate nature of beauty will be unclear if its relations to the nature of the good and the true are not understood. There exists, then, an 'idée du beau,' which

5

is an absolute truth by which God manifests himself; and it is related to the absolute truths of the good, of mathematics, etc. Just like those truths, the idea of beauty is attained by a process of 'abstraction immédiate,' an immediate grasping of the absolute. And though the knowledge of beauty is experienced differently from that of the other absolute truths, still

> Si le vrai, le beau et le bien nous paraissent distincts, ce n'est pas qu'ils le soient en effet, mais c'est qu'ils nous sont donnés dans des objets différents. Le vrai existe par soi-même; réalisé dans les actions humaines, il devient le bien; engagé sous les formes sensibles, il devient le beau.[6]

There exists an absolute idea of beauty, which, just as in the understanding of the ideas of the true and the good, can be realized only in a concrete circumstance. The creative artist, or 'génie,' must enclose his absolute idea in some particular material envelope. This does not mean that the idea is first conceived, and then some matter found to represent it. Rather, as in the case of all cognitive experiences, the concrete and the absolute are grasped simultaneously, and each understood by means of the other. The aim of art is 'expression,' the revelation through matter of the spirit which informs it, which is its fullest meaning. Cousin writes:

> La beauté physique ou la beauté des formes et des mouvements, n'est qu'un reflet de la beauté morale et intellectuelle, que nous pouvons comprendre sous le seul terme de beauté spirituelle ou immatérielle....[7]

The criterion for judging art lies in the question whether or not the artistic medium adequately represents the idea lying behind it. The idea which is to be concretely expressed will be that of absolute beauty, but it will also be that of goodness and of truth. The ideas of the good and true will likewise contain that of the beautiful: a noble action will strike us as beautiful; so will a mathematical solution. But the basic unity of these absolute

6

ideas must not be attributed to the manner in which they are reached. The artist's experience in fusing idea with material content is different in kind from that of a mathematician solving a problem, or of a saint following his duty. Only if his aesthetic experience is pure, i.e. derived solely from the idea of beauty, will the artist be able to create beauty.

Cousin devotes some attention to the theories proposed to explain the nature of the beauty which art realizes in matter. He rejects a number of them before bringing in his own cognitive argument. The sensual theory, the utility theory, the theory based on the co-ordination of elements, or on the order and harmony of parts, are all eliminated. The sensual theory is carefully attacked. Its error, Cousin thinks, is to have confused the beautiful with the sensually agreeable. The fact is that the art which is most moving is often least agreeable sensually, while the most attractive sensually excludes genuine aesthetic experience and feeling. The condition of calm repose which accompanies aesthetic experience is absent from any sense-experience, which is always more or less subject to passion. The theory that art seems beautiful because it is useful is easily shown to be incomplete: the most useful objects are ugly, and the most beautiful are useless in any practical sense. The theory that beauty is order, or composition, Cousin dismisses as being superficial, though the nearest to truth. Those objects in which a very obvious symmetry is dominant do not for that reason strike us as more beautiful than those, a rose, the ocean, in which the existence of order, while certain, is not obvious. Cousin proposes unity in variety as the basic characteristic of beauty in objects. By this, he seems to mean that in genuine art there are two separable, though closely related, elements: a group of qualities, or attributes; and an essence. This essence might be called the 'spiritual center' of a work of art, and as such furnishes the unity of tone which makes the work one. That beauty is captured by this definition and eludes the theory of proportion, or composition, is shown by comparing beauty,

7

properly speaking, with a more intense form of itself, sublimity. The sublime, which exceeds the grasp of the senses, while remaining intelligible to reason, gives high aesthetic pleasure despite the fact that it offends man's natural sense of proportion. The reason for this pleasure is that there is a grand and strong unity which affords the center for the overwhelming variety in the experience of the sublime.

This unity, which is essential to the work of art, functions with the diversity, or liveliness of the work to account for its identity and its reality. The essence or unity of the work seems, in Cousin's thought, especially related to a kind of 'beauté morale' which is a proper part of every genuinely aesthetic object. Of the three general classes of beauty in objects, physical beauty, intellectual beauty, and moral beauty, the last is the most profound, and is shared in some degree by the two others. It should be noticed, by the way, that these three classes of beauty, and especially the moral, are all found equally in actions, objects, or artistic representations of objects. It is because of this moral quality of aesthetic experience that there is more perfect beauty in man than in the animals (or in representations of either), and more beauty in any animate creature than in any inanimate one. In one curious passage, admittedly, Cousin does argue for the equally great moral expressiveness of nature:

> Je dis que la face de la nature est expressive comme la face de l'homme. Si la figure de la femme nous paraît belle, parce qu'elle est le reflet de la douceur et de la bonté, n'est-ce-pas aussi un caractère de bienveillance et de grandeur qui fait la beauté de la lumière du soleil?[8]

In general, though, he argues that the less material beauty is, the more spiritual, hence essential, hence nearly ideal it is, and that materiality is greatest in nature, least great in man among created things. As man is fundamentally a moral being, it is natural that this quality should be sharply revealed in the best artistic representations or descriptions of him, and it is this quality which, diffused through a work, gives it its unity.

All of these considerations of the beautiful in objects are only half comprehensible without an understanding of Cousin's theory of the beautiful 'dans l'esprit de l'homme.' This theory is the counterpart of his spiritualistic notion that unity in variety accounts for the beauty within an artistic object. The mind, he contends, contains two faculties which are related to beauty, namely 'goût' and 'génie.' Both faculties operate through the exercise of imagination, but in the case of 'génie,' a creative power, some undefinable activity is present which is lacking to 'goût,' which is only an appreciative, sensitive power. Of 'génie' Cousin writes:

> Le génie est avant tout inventeur et créateur. L'homme de génie n'est pas le maître de la force qui est en lui; c'est par le besoin ardent, irrésistible, d'exprimer ce qu'il éprouve, qu'il est homme de génie.[9]

'Goût,' which is the faculty of judging beauty, is much more subject to rational control than is 'génie.' Of the sensitive 'goût,' Cousin writes:

> La plus haute culture qu'on puisse donner au goût, c'est la culture du sentiment du beau; il faut s'exercer sans cesse à briser les enveloppes matérielles pour arriver à la beauté morale.[10]

'Goût,' therefore, is in harmony with that particular spiritual beauty which gives unity to objects. It involves the passing of a judgment which is naturally reached by spontaneous comparison, or co-realization, of the particular material representation of beauty with the absolute idea of beauty as dictated to the mind by 'raison.'[11] Before formulating this theory, however, Cousin eliminates the false theories of 'le beau dans l'esprit de l'homme.' His refutation of the sensualist theory is again based on its confusion of the agreeable with the beautiful. The theory which explains beauty as a 'sentiment' is more satisfactory than the sensualist theory, and accounts for one basic fact of aesthetic experience. It is true that in the rational judgment of the beauty

9

of an object, there is an accompanying feeling of 'amour' for that object, though it is subordinate to the judgment it accompanies. This sentiment is quite distinct from passion.

> Le sentiment du beau, libre de tout désir et en même temps de toute crainte, élève et échauffe l'âme, et peut la transporter jusqu'à l'enthousiasme, sans lui faire connaître les troubles de la passion.[12]

This 'sentiment' is raised to the level of sublimity when a very vast object is presented. At that time, intellect or 'raison' is able to comprehend the object and judge it, but the senses are unable to take in all its aspects, so are obliged to struggle and extend themselves. The emotion aroused is intense, but purely aesthetic. The sentimental theory contributes to the full understanding of beauty in the mind. By itself, though, this theory is variable, and cannot be reduced to any basic, unchanging principles. The rational judgment of the beauty of an object, which is fundamental to 'goût' or in the activity of 'génie,' is imagination. It is, as Cousin puts it, the association of 'sentiment' with the faculties of the mind: it is love united with memory, with will, and with reason. Memory operates to recall, at will, previous images or sensations. Then, without a certain 'feeling' for the object, that object will not seem genuinely beautiful. It is plain that the imagination will operate more intensively in the creative artist, the 'génie,' than in the appreciator of a work of art, but in both cases imagination has the same component parts, and operates in the same way.

The 'génie' is in the power of a force stronger than himself, which makes him express his aesthetic feelings. There is, though, nothing haphazard about his action in the control of this force. Because of the paradox in Cousin's thought, by which the most rational thought, i.e. thought informed by 'raison,' is acquired by spontaneous realization of absolute truth, it is possible to say that the intensely driven activity of the 'génie' is adequate to the highest kind of cognition. The creative artist realizes his imaginative conception simultaneously with a realization of the absolute idea of beauty. Therefore his creation partakes of both 'le beau idéal' and 'le beau réel.' In this sense, then, Cousin means that art improves on nature. The artist expresses the spiritual, ideal content in nature, along with its diversity and particularity. There can be no doubt, though, that the artist loses much of the vitality in nature, and his accomplishment is only an improvement over nature in a wholly different realm. Practically considered, his improvement is to have distilled the dross out of life and to have created an ideal, virtuous rendering of nature.[13] In this sense Cousin exalts the creative artist, is able to say that art is, in its own right, a kind of religion, and that the artist is a kind of priest. The absolute truth which he attains is a manifestation of God.

The different arts can be classified, and to a degree ranked, by their material abilities to express the genius' conceptions of ideal beauty. Only the arts which are directed to vision and hearing are genuinely 'expressive.' This tenet furnishes the major principle of division. Within this broad division, Cousin recognizes a principle of classification in terms of freedom or limitation. The least free arts are those of gardening and architecture, the mediums of which are hardly tractable at all. Music is the freest of the arts, and is profound by means of its vagueness and its suggestiveness. It is characteristic of an art of pure sound that it is profoundly evocative. Poetry, the most profound and meaningful of all the arts, is superior to music because its free suggestiveness is controlled by a symbol, the word, which is far more precise, i.e., capable of being conceptualized, than musical notation. Among the superior plastic arts, sculpture is as precise and determinable as music is vague, and for that reason lacks something of the profundity involved in vagueness. Painting is conceived to combine the tangibility of sculpture with the vagueness of music, but to fall below the more rationalizable art of poetry.

Cousin's emphasis on the contrast of the determinate with the indeterminate is interesting. He believes that the suggesting of infinity is a necessary element in the profundity of an art. It is true that he criticizes music for being nebulous: he devotes some critical discussion to the fact that several listeners can reach no agreement about the kind of scene or situation being 'depicted' by a piece of music. But what he considers an excess of richness in music becomes, under control, the main key to the greatness of poetry. The 'indéterminé,' which is immediately and profoundly reached by poetry, is distinct from the non-determined quality of the absolute ideas, a quality of freedom from any local conditions. And the infinite towards which poetry yearns is not described in the same way as the infinite which is God, the source of the idea of beauty. God, whether conceived chiefly as substance, or as chiefly cause and identical with the totality of the created world, is always a logical induction from the absolute, rational ideas by which he manifests himself. The 'infini déterminé' toward which poetry strives, Cousin's notion of logical abstraction notwithstanding, is not a concept which is instantly and simply attained. The response evoked by the experience of poetry ascends rather toward a realm of cloudy spiritual feelings.

> La parole humaine, idéalisée par la poésie, a la profondeur et l'éclat de la note musicale; et elle est lumineuse autant que pathétique: elle parle à l'esprit comme au cœur; elle est en cela inimitable, unique, qu'elle rassemble en elle tous les extrêmes et tous les contraires, dans une harmonie qui redouble leur effet, et où tour à tour paraissent et se développent toutes les images, tous les sentiments, toutes les idées, toutes les facultés humaines, tous les replis de l'âme, toutes les faces des choses, tous les mondes réels et tous les mondes intelligibles.[14]

Poetry, then, ravishes both reason and emotion, drawing them toward the absolute source of beauty, and at the same time drawing up to an ideal realm all of the contingent reality of the world to which the poet has given form. In his discussions of all the arts, Cousin holds that the experiencing of them is a fusion both of the reflectively rational and spontaneously rational

12

aspects of mind. He never claims a similar fusion in the experiencing of the moral law or elsewhere. And in the experience of the moral law, he states, the particular experience is instantly apodictic, and provides a perfectly clear decision as to the choice which will should make. To be sure, in his discussion of the 'beau réel' and the 'beau idéal,' which co-exist in every aesthetic experience, he affirms that the absolute aesthetic law is immediately apprehended; but he is driven toward making his interpretation of this experience much more nearly metaphorical and suggestive in his treatment of aesthetic. Similar enrichment appears in his notion of unity and variety as the component elements of beauty in objects. He distinguishes his notion from that of order, or proportion, because he means something different from a merely structural criterion for beauty. His criterion is the presence, within the diverse elements of a work, of a certain spiritual essence, in experiencing which one attains the 'idea' of both goodness and beauty. The creator of that spiritually unified work is a non-reflecting, though rational, victim of a greater force, the force to create. And this force is simply an intensification of the 'amour' which links the appreciator of an art object to that object.

L'homme de goût doit posséder l'amour éclairé mais ardent de la beauté: if faut qu'il se complaise à la rencontrer, qu'il la cherche, qu'il l'appelle. Comprendre et démontrer qu'une chose n'est point belle, plaisir médiocre, tâche ingrate; mais discerner une belle chose, s'en pénétrer, la mettre en évidence et faire partager à d'autres son sentiment, jouissance exquise, tâche généreuse.[15]

# III

During a suspension from teaching, 1820-1828, Cousin made a complete translation of Plato; it remained standard throughout the nineteenth century. The work was praised for its natural recapturing of the Platonic style, and its insight into the shadings of Plato's thought. Not only was Cousin deeply informed about Platonism, but his own original thought, which constantly returns to that master, prepared him to understand Plato. He continually looked to the authority of the doctrine of ideas, and in his older age, when he returned to a vague spiritualism, he found himself giving a superficial expression to a more or less profound Platonism which had underlain all of his thought. Janet has written:

> Comme il avait commencé, il a fini par Platon; l'idéalisme platoni-cien a été le nœud et le centre de toute sa carrière philosophique.[16]

In the heart of the Platonic aesthetic tradition, in the Doctrine of Ideas, is a dominant trait not only of Cousin's aesthetic but of his whole philosophy. This is the conception of a realm of unchanging ideas, which are the essences of their reflections here on earth, and which are the only 'reals.' I overlook here the problem of the kind of reality of the realm of those 'ideas,' and will only mention their ontological 'nature.' My chief documents will be the untechnical *Phaedrus* and *Symposium*. But

14

it must be remembered, and recalled later, that Cousin's conception of the 'idées absolues' is of a quite different sort from Plato's. For Cousin the ideas are eternal and objective manifestations of God's thought. They are attained simply and immediately, through a spontaneous abstraction, 'abstraction immédiate.' Cousin's conception of the kind of existence of the ideas, and of the way they are known, is not qualitative, or nuancé. It is precisely their qualitative description as aspects of experience which gives Plato's 'Ideas' and the cognition of them their distinctive aesthetic significance.

Still the general conception of Ideas, and the way of explaining the experience of them, is a fundamental notion which Cousin inherited from Plato. While Plato's entire positive conception of beauty passed over to Cousin in some form, within the doctrine of Ideas, the association of the ideas of goodness and truth with beauty chiefly marks Cousin's aesthetic as Platonic. When I come to consider his relation to the aesthetic theory of his time, it will be clear why this association is a major debt of Cousin to Plato. A central problem of the history of aesthetic concerns the relation of beauty to goodness and truth. In its Platonic form the elements of this problem are fused in the nature of the experience of the beautiful. In its Horatian, and neoclassical form, with its *utile-dulce* opposition, a work of art is presumed to offer two distinct values; the combination of them is supposed to combine their qualities, but in fact they are unfusible, the *utile* being conceived as practical in the sense of preparing for proper doing, while the *dulce* is a source merely of passive pleasure. In its treatment by German idealist aesthetic, beauty is an informing by the Geist of its own unconscious, 'natural' past; it is a manifestation of truth in sensuous art, and a 'good' in the sense which that word can have in Hegelian philosophy, i.e., as a mode of spiritual existence. The aesthetic of the second Romantic generation, chiefly that of 'l'art-pour-l'art,' was the heir, even when unknowingly, to these problems of defining and situating the nature of the experience of beauty, and thereby of deter-

15

mining the position which the experience of the beautiful holds between ethical and logical experience. The answer given by 'l'art-pour-l'art,' and suggested in Cousin, is that beauty, meaning only artistic beauty, rebels at being employed to rational or ethical ends, or to being considered as a kind of sense-experience. When left alone, art, the worship of beauty, can be 'une sorte de religion à lui-même,' good, beautiful, and true. The philosophic justification of this idea, which passed from Cousin to the first French romantics, has its roots in the Platonic solution.

It would be disorderly, though, to take up Plato's doctrinal notion of the relation of the idea of beauty to other ideas before noticing two other aspects of Plato's conception of beauty; they are both related to his doctrine of Ideas, and introductory to it. One of those aspects, that of a beautiful 'harmony,' nourished later Platonism, and found its way into Cousin's thought. The other aspect, Plato's too often disparaged attack on art, contributed negatively, as I want to show first, to an elevated doctrine of 'aesthetic semblance,' which was to be strengthened throughout the Platonic tradition, passing through Plotinus and Shaftesbury, and ultimately reaching Cousin.

Plato hesitated about the kind of value to assign to the experience of beauty, whether to consider it cognition or simply opinion. This because of his misgivings about art. He held that much art is a kind of sensuous deception, one remove farther away from 'ideal' reality than is the nature which it imitates. For this reason he could not justify the place of many examples of art – as it then existed – in his ideal society. Plato did not grant art the power of effecting even the same enrichment of the whole person which takes place in other experiences of beauty. And the creative artistic soul, he thought, is not reliably intelligent. In the *Apology*, when the poet is inspired, he composes by means of μανία, not of φύσις, and so is unable to explain the meaning of his work. Plato makes a similar complaint against Ion: he is an undiscriminating mouthpiece of divine inspiration, and can never be a rational citizen; though Plato elsewhere admires as a kind of cognition the divine μανία which strikes such as Ion. Evidence for Plato's hostility to poets and poetry – as they then existed – abounds, and much exists for his suspicion toward the other 'imitative' arts.  The evidence reduces mainly to the argument that imitative artists do not deal with reality, and that they deal with their copies of reality in an irrational way, which can therefore not be used for the properly guided education of citizens.

So 'ideal beauty,' in its relation to good and truth, is by no means reached in most artistic experience.  But there is more: in passing from Plato's views of art to a more positive aspect of his ideas of beauty, there is a danger of overlooking a significance in his very negative notion of imitative art itself.  This is the suggestion of the theory of 'aesthetic semblance' from which virtually all progress in subsequent art-theory followed.  The suggestion, which Bosanquet points out clearly, is that art is distinct from nature, and that the faculty by which art is experienced differs from that by which nature is perceived.  Furthermore, the thought that art and the artist simply create copies is rich, because, as Bosanquet says,

> When Plato insists that the appearances employed by the artist are in relation not with the unseen world of thought and law, but with a lower reality which is itself only an image of that unseen world, it is impossible not to observe in this a strong though negative suggestion of the function of beauty as a symbol for spiritual things.[17]

And, as he goes on to recall, in the *Timaeus* Plato actually says that the creator made the world beautiful by modelling it on an underlying order.  It remained for others to argue that art and artists are uniquely qualified to reveal that beauty which is order or harmony.  This argument is basic to the Platonic tradition; it can also be seen in Plotinus and Shaftesbury.  It is an argument which, in the Platonic aesthetic tradition, will never be more than a part of a larger conception, which relates beauty to all goodness and truth, whether or not they are found in art.

Plato's own positive conception of beauty is not one which explains the creative relation of artist and art to nature. It considers beauty in two major and closely related aspects: its relation to love and its relation to education. In both cases, the experience of beauty is a kind of un-rational cognition. The rhythm followed in the experience of beauty is that dialectical one which underlies the movement of Plato's thought, and which, like the dialectic of romantic idealism, is, in a sense, the process which it describes. So, in Plato's conception of beauty in education, it is an interactive, progressive harmony between the soul of the one being educated, and some educating element, music, teaching, etc., which is for the youth a process of truth-gaining. The experience of beauty as an object of educated love involves a growing understanding of, hence wishing for, more spiritual objects of love.

Plato believes that beauty is important but dangerous in education. If the soul is exposed to the wrong kind of beauty, its own inner harmony may be disrupted. In the *Philebus* he distinguishes between the mixed and pure pleasures of the soul. The mixed pleasures are those which satisfy a lack, and might be compared to the scratching of itches; such pleasures are common in drama or poetry. Pure pleasures are caused by simple shapes, simple colors, and the hearing of single musical notes or simple rhythms. Such experiences awaken a harmony in the soul corresponding, somehow, to the harmony which is the cause of the pleasure. It has been pointed out, by Bosanquet, that the cognitive aspect of Greek aesthetic never goes beyond certain metaphors of unity in variety or geometrical simplicity, and it is just such qualities which, when perceived by the harmonious soul, provide the basis for the kind of pure pleasure described above.[18]

Bosanquet also claims that the metaphor of the 'beautiful soul,' which springs out of this supposedly real spiritual harmony between the affected observer and the work of art, exceeds the limits of an aesthetic statement. But for my purposes it is

18

important to see to what extent Plato's conception of beauty is founded on this fundamentally non-artistic basis.

In the *Republic* and *Laws*, where Plato is especially anxious to define the proper education of a citizen, the profound influence of art on the soul is implied by the great caution with which art is treated. The main end for every citizen is goodness, and goodness is a mode of being which can coincide with the experiencing of beauty. This is true because Plato's aesthetic is simple in such a way that to experience beauty is to be beautiful.[19] And beauty resides in that same harmony which is the essence of the soul, the seat of goodness. As a marginal note to the *Philebus* observes:

> The principle of goodness has reduced itself to the law of beauty. For measure and proportion always pass into beauty and excellence.[20]

As proportion resides in simplicity, and the nourishment of a beautiful rhythm in the soul, it is simple and repeatedly experienced music which Plato thinks the best educative art.[21] He says:

> And is it not for this reason, Glaucon, that education in music is most sovereign, because more than anything else rhythm and harmony find their way to the inmost soul and take strongest hold upon it, bringing with them and imparting grace, if one is rightly trained, and otherwise the contrary![22]

The end of music, then, is not to give pleasure, but to 'inform' the soul. Plato tends not to conceive of an aesthetic pleasure, or interest, which is independent of interest in the objects themselves which are represented. Hence music, the least representative art, is the beauty which is least dangerous. In light of the effect which 'music' has on the young, it is clear how much Plato's conception of it reflects the generally educative sense which the Greeks gave to that term. He conceives of it, actually, as a kind of acquired, or 'imitated' rhythm, by which man reveals the spiritual influences which he has experienced. It is the kind of general form which Pater describes when he writes that

19

Philosophy itself, indeed, as he (Plato) conceives it, is but the sympathetic appreciation of a kind of music in the very nature of things.[23]

On the hypothesis of a harmony pervading man's soul, pervading things outside man, and the structure of the universe, Plato accounts for the experience of beauty, and the union of beauty and goodness, at least in his educational theory. It is in his Doctrine of Ideas that the union of intelligible goodness and beauty is to be found most clearly and in a form which most bears on Cousin's thought. The 'harmonic' conception of beauty cannot be isolated from Plato's conception in the Doctrine of Ideas (either as it affects Cousin, or as it is to be found in Plato). For Plato, the bridge between the two conceptions is to be found in the nature of the experience of beauty. This experience always takes place in the soul, and the essential quality of the soul is to be in motion. The soul always moves toward that which is most fully like it: that which is most spiritual. This affinity of spirit for spirit is love. It is this kind of love by which the soul rises to the supreme beauty, the Idea of Beauty, which is most nearly like itself, through becoming progressively spiritualized in each stage of ascension. Such love by affinity depends on the same essential harmony pervading the lover and beloved, as that which pervades both the simply proportioned beautiful example of art and the soul of the lover of that work of art. Once this particular relation between the Doctrine of Ideas, and the theory of aesthetic harmony, has been described, it is easy to see how in both cases beauty and good are united. They are integrated in the experience involved. As in the case of harmonious education, so in the case of love, beauty and goodness are the single objects of a complex cognition, which has been well called 'cognitive desire,' and which might also be called 'passionate reason.' The myths of the *Phaedrus* and *Symposium* attempt to define this cognition.

The nature of this Platonic cognition is of great importance here. Cousin admires the Platonic theory of the ascension to true beauty, which is described in the *Symposium*, although his own central 'théorie de la raison' offers a different explanation, one which betrays his debt to neoclassisicm. He conceives of the 'beau idéal' as the essence and moral 'idea' which underlies the particular, changeable beauty that is experienced by sense. This ideal beauty is cognized by the 'abstraction immédiate' which 'raison' operates on the particular beauties. Though Cousin does not claim that the ideal beauty is completely realized by each cognition, still his description of the 'beau idéal' makes it difficult to explain how each different 'real' beauty is related, in a way unique to it, with an ideal beauty which is ultimately a substantial unity, the 'Idée du Beau.' But Plato's theory of the ascension to the Idea of Beauty shares with Cousin's notion the belief that beauty is essentially moral; if not that the beautifully moral is attained by abstraction. For Plato, the reality of the Idea of Beauty is cognized only after a careful training in the perception of less spiritual, but still real, beauties. Each particular beauty which is perceived is logically grounded in the Idea of Beauty, and may point toward it ,but has its entire being within itself. It is either a memory of that Idea or a foreshadowing of it.

That love of the beautiful which memory, 'anamnesis,' awakens, is first a love of the good. The good is the object of all human desire:

οὐδέν γε ἄλλο ἐστὶν οὗ ἐρῶσιν ἄνθρωποι ἢ τοῦ ἀγαθοῦ.

And:

ἔρως τοῦ τὸ ἀγαθὸν αὐτῷ εἶναι ἀεί.[24]

It has been said that the beautiful is simply 'la spendeur du bien,' in Plato's thought. As it is the good which is the universal object of wisdom, only ignorance can lead a man not to pursue the good, and thus the beautiful. The particular interest which leads man to pursue the beautiful is the desire to procreate in beauty, whether his offspring are children or fine deeds and thoughts. The cognition of beauty is not, however, 'interested,' in the sense of pursuing the satisfaction of sense-desires. It is a form of contemplation which has no end but itself. The feeling of pleasure is not essential to this contemplation. J. A. Stewart has called its condition that of a 'fairly prolonged intermittent reverie,' for it seems to hold its objects in a kind of dream-state, both real and unreal as objects are in such cognition. In this sense it is possible to call the beautiful the object of 'cognitive desire.' The order of cognitions of the beautiful is from the least to the most spiritual objects. The *Phaedrus* explains how the soul, which has once seen the realm of ideas, forever longs for that beauty, as it is found in love-worthy humans. In the *Symposium*, the order of loving begins with the beautiful person, and passes through beautiful forms, then ideas, to the immutable beauty, which is seldom reached. This ascension through 'knowing' and 'desiring' is an experience of the whole person, much like the experience of the choral dance which integrates the motions both of bodily and intellectual 'reason.'

This notion is obviously different from Cousin's theory of 'abstraction immédiate' to a 'Beau Idéal.' The neoclassical aesthetic which lies behind Cousin's conception is vitiated by its stress, always modified in some sense, on reason as a distinct, adjudicating faculty of the mind. In his aesthetic, Cousin includes 'raison' as a component in the imagination, and in the experience of 'goût.' An undiscursive 'raison' is the keystone of his metaphysics. This faculty has the appearance of intuition, but is actually an impersonal substance giving identical conceptual knowledge to all men. Plato's case is totally other: even if he had not been heir to the Hellenic tradition of 'musical' culture, the vital harmony which he imagined to ground every aesthetic experience would have prevented association of such experience with any aspect of reason. Since the experience of beauty, for Plato, is a 'process' within life, it must be described in qualitative terms. This may explain why the Idea of Beauty plays little part in the logical structure of the Doctrine of Ideas and serves rather as a magnet drawing up all particular ex-

22

periences of beauty. In the same fashion, each particular beauty on the spiritual scale attracts a lover by means of an intermediary daemon. This Eros or Daemon, which mediates between the lover and the beloved beauty in the *Symposium*, is absent in the conception by which Cousin, in his 'théorie de la raison,' relates particular aesthetic experience to its archetypal 'idée du beau.' The absence is significant both because Cousin depends on Plato for his notion of absolute ideas, and because he pays homage elsewhere to the Platonic notion of ascension through progressively spiritual beauties to the supreme beauty.

In his analysis of Platonic idealism, in the *Cours de l'Histoire de la Philosophie moderne*, 1829, Cousin provides the key to his peculiar misunderstanding of Plato. He writes that

> le procédé constant de Platon est l'abstraction, et l'abstraction lui donne une tendance idéale.[25]

The reason for this direction of interpretation will be clear later: in light of Cousin's debt to Quatremère de Quincy. For Quincy the ideal beauty is that intellectual interpretation of nature which represents the essential, generalized truths in nature, truths which are involved in but veiled to sense experience. The ideal model for the artist must be a sort of essential abstraction, by which the artist gives form to the 'diversité insignifiante' of nature. Under the sway of this theory, Cousin goes on:

> en esthétique, dans un bel objet, il (Platon) sépare sévèrement la matière du beau, qui est apparente, visible, tangible, sensible enfin, de la beauté elle-même, qui ne tombe pas sous nos sens, qui n'est pas une image, mais une idée, et c'est à cette beauté idéale, qu'il rapporte l'amour.[26]

Here is Cousin's error. Plato does not 'severely separate' the material from the spiritual elements in a beautiful object. He could hardly have done this: for in considering non-artistic objects as supremely beautiful, on the whole, he was not concerned with any form-matter relationships. What Plato argued was that the degree of spiritual harmony, love of the beautiful, obtaining between lover and beloved beautiful object, is the measure of the 'beauty' of the experience. Cousin failed to distinguish between this realistic 'cognitive desire' for the spiritual, in Plato, and a theory drawn primarily from neoclassical art-critics, which held for an ideal, spiritualized essence as the perfection of each 'real beauty'; so he wrongly attributed to Plato the belief that the Idea of Beauty is a more or less active and superior component in every aesthetic experience. He is assimilating Plato to his own position. In 'Du Beau Réel et du Beau Idéal' he writes:

> Primitivement le beau réel nous est donné comme composé de particulier et de général, de relatif, et d'absolu, de variété et d'unité. L'abstraction immédiate, en dégageant l'absolu du relatif, lui rend sa pureté et sa simplicité, et l'idéal est trouvé.[27]

I remarked that Cousin's notion of the closeness of Beauty and Goodness was a major debt to Plato and the Platonic tradition. This notion, just as that of ascension through spiritual beauty, took a new turn in Cousin's thought. He confuses Plato's ascension with the neoclassical 'beau-idéal' theory, so deprives it of its original 'reality.' Thus the union of beauty and goodness, which Plato integrates in the very experience of beauty, as well as in the realm of Ideas, has less coherence in Cousin. He owes to Plato the conception of the Ideas of Beauty and Goodness as transcendently identical, but finds that the way those ideas are co-experienced in the experience of 'real' beauty is hard to explain on the 'beau-réel,' 'beau-idéal' theory. While adapting Plato's moral theory of beauty, Cousin never appreciated just how non-artistic Plato's aesthetic was. While Cousin attributes beauty to actions, mathematical solutions, etc., the absence from them of any proper form-content, ideal-real dichotomy prevents him from analyzing the nature of their 'beauty.' As they, and their like, are the most evident examples of the experienced fusion of goodness and beauty, the neglect of them forces Cousin to leave their particular beauty-goodness composition in a kind

24

of formal juxtaposition, dictated by participation in their respective 'ideas.' But when not considering these elements explicitly in the light of the real-ideal dualism in which they exist and are experienced, Cousin affirms an integral aesthetic union of beauty and goodness.

Plato always conceives the love of beauty as a moral love. Cousin introduces a similar thought by his insistence that all beauty is 'symbolique' and even 'sympathique'. By this he means that all 'real' beauty basically expresses moral qualities in terms of physical qualities. He writes that the end of art is the expression of moral beauty in terms of physical beauty. The latter is only an artistic symbol of the former. The same relation holds for the beauty found in nature. Taste is appreciative, Cousin says: it is the moral faculty of man in the presence of the moral in nature; man judges whether the natural symbol is appropriate to its moral idea. And again, Cousin argues that even the beauty of the sun results from some inexplicable expression of moral qualities, of 'bonté.' Within the realm of 'real beauties' there are three main classes: physical, intellectual, and moral. The unity and virtue of them all resides in their more or less veiled expression, or 'symbolization,' of spiritually moral beauties. This conception of an ascension through moral beauties resembles the Platonic conception found in the *Symposium*.

The Platonic conception is continued in Plotinus and Shaftesbury. But it is superficially distinct from its successors. Within Cousin, all of these beauties are simply 'beautés réelles,' not the ideal beauty with which they are supposed to be co-experienced. In the Platonic tradition, on the other hand, these beauties are not only real, but, as is clear in Plotinus, are of the essence of reality. So the distinction which Cousin makes is significant, though he never closely faces it. He seems to apply even to moral, natural, or intellectual beauty the 'beau-réel' 'beau-idéal' standard; odd as that seems in this case. The problem is this: that he has imported a neoclassical artistic distinction into the chiefly non-artistic aesthetic of Plato and his tradition. Thus while Cousin shares with Plato the idea of a harmonic bond drawing the observer to the morally beautiful object – a bond which integrates goodness and beauty – while, for Cousin, a fusion of goodness and beauty takes place on the level of 'real' beauty, it is left open that a 'more' real experience of this fusion might take place on the ideal level. In his 1853 edition of *Du Vrai, Du Beau, et Du Bien*, Cousin asserts that this fusion operates equally in both ideal and real beauty, in both of which God, the beautiful and good, is adumbrated. Still the influence of Plato's notion of harmony, on Cousin's early aesthetic, should be limited to a notion of 'moral sympathy' which Cousin holds between the three classes of 'real' beauty and man. But this true evaluative aesthetic, which measures beauty by its degree of moral expressiveness, is a deep contribution of Plato to Cousin. Also Platonic is the description of the 'sentiment' which is felt in the moral sympathy of observer with beautiful object. Cousin writes that it is

> un sentiment exquis d'amour pur et désintéressé[28]

and says that it provides

> une joie douce et tranquille, une sorte d'épanouissement.[29]

In such descriptions, and in many others, Cousin shows his natural affinity for Plato, unmixed with conflicting influences.

Finally, it would be misleading to overlook the interest of Cousin in the *Hippias Major*, a dialogue questionably attributed to Plato. Cousin considers it a fine source for refutations of false cognitive theories of beauty. The form of it, the brief refutations by Socrates of Hippias' ideas on beauty, has plainly passed over into Cousin's rhetorical tactic in two chapters of his 1853 edition of *Du Vrai, Du Beau, et Du Bien*. In the dialogue Socrates forces Hippias to look for a beauty which is independent of any particular beauties, and which exists as their cause; in order, Socrates rejects the suggestion that beauty is the useful, or

26

that which is pleasing through sight and hearing. No conclusion is reached about what beauty is. Cousin, too, rejects these theories. The one he chooses, that of unity in variety, is latent in Plato's thought. Such unity Plato conceives metaphorically, in terms of the soul-body relation, or of the harmonious functioning of different elements in the unit of the body. Cousin never presses the problem farther than this.

One of the main aesthetic problems is the definition of the nature of aesthetic experience relative to ethical and logical experience. Plato's aesthetic experience subsumes the other two kinds of experience in itself. The Platonic aesthetic is deeply non-eudaemonistic. It will sanction only beauty which is experienced as cognition and pure love. Cousin follows the Platonic fusion of goodness and truth with beauty on two different levels. In terms of his 'idées absolues' – the most obviously Platonic elements in his thought – he holds that the Idea of Beauty, present in all aesthetic experience, is implicitly identical with the ideas of Goodness and Truth. Further, he holds that in the experiencing of 'real beauty' a basically moral 'sentiment' binds the observer to the morally beautiful object, idea, or act. The value of moral beauty lies, for Plato, in its degree of spiritual elevation, and the ascension to higher beauty is through the cognitive desire described throughout his writings. Cousin adapts that same ascension, while confusing with it, and placing alongside it, his own neoclassical doctrine of the 'beau idéal.' In Cousin's work these two unharmonized principles depreciate 'real,' in the sense of material, beauty, and set before all 'real' beauty some higher form of beauty. In Cousin's spiritualistic 1853 edition of *Du Vrai, Du Beau, et Du Bien*, he argues that the 'beau idéal' and the beauty reached by ascension through 'real' spiritual beauties are basically the same, each having God as its immediate 'terme.' It seems that Cousin returns at last to the deep-felt Platonism which all along underlies his discursive thinking.

Cousin knew later Greek philosophy thoroughly. During the period between 1820-28, when he was suspended from teaching, he undertook not only his complete translation of Plato, but a complete edition of Proclus; and, no doubt, most of the work for his *Nouveaux Fragments Philosophiques*, which appeared in 1828, with critical – largely historical and textual – essays on Eunapius, Proclus, and Olympiodorus. The practical complexities of the period, the need to interpret scanty data, to establish plausible texts, and to trace the involutions of the first 'scholastic' thought, clearly attracted Cousin. He stands at the head of those 19th century thinkers who were fascinated by the mythological eclecticism of the Alexandrians. This study deeply influenced Cousin's own philosophy.

He probably did not realize the profound effect of Plotinus on all later aesthetic, including neoclassical theories from which he himself drew, Plotinus' great aesthetic advance was to have followed the argument by which Plato depreciated art, and there to have found the most general significance of art. Plato had said that art is a copy of a copy. Plotinus said that art copies only in the sense of interpreting the meaning which lies under the phenomena of nature. Plato's confusion stems from his doubt that 'material' beauty can symbolize the meaning of 'spiritual' truth, as well as from non-metaphysical suspicions about the practical use of art.

Plotinus' correction of Plato is rooted deeply in his systematized Platonism. Plotinus conceives the universe as a pattern of emanations and 'epistrophes.' By a necessity, which is the freedom of self-determination, the One emanates Divine Reason, the σπερματικοὶ λόγοι, the logical structure of the Ideas or archetypes of the world, which in turn emanates the world-soul and individual souls, which, finally, emanate matter, in greater or less purity. What results is a 'great chain of being,' every link of which yearns to return, to be fused to the more spiritual link just above it. This because, in its act of original self-division, the One had introduced into the realm of being the first elements, the Ideas, of slightly diminished being. With each descending level, the substance in question suffered an ontological loss. That is to

28

say, it became more mixed with matter, which Plotinus considers non-being, and which plays a great part in Plotinus' theory of ugliness. All created things long to return to the One, as that means, practically, to be as fully themselves as they can, thereby realizing their being, or spiritual natures, or 'essential forms.' No aspect of nature is so spiritless that it has no wish for redemption, or existence. The world of physical nature is instinct with unconscious and longing form. The potential artist, likewise, is instinct with never fully purified form. When he observes mute nature he may, having a natural affinity to the spiritual power in nature, which reminds him of his own soul, desire to express the submerged form of nature. This he does by a sort of conspiracy: of his own inner cognition of his own utmost spiritual form, the σπερματικοὶ λόγοι, with an intuition of the half-expressed form of nature. There results a spiritual creation which, if beautiful, is ontologically superior to nature, though it is nature itself, in the fullest sense. Its spiritual form will be the measure of the beauty of such a creation. In this way Plotinus vindicates art against Plato's metaphysical attack, and without evading the issue, for he considers art as fully realized within the materially beautiful object. At the same time, as Bosanquet points out, Plotinus frees art from the limits of the moralistic criticism which Plato directed at the objects which art 'copies.' For Plotinus, clearly, the objects 'copied' by art are less 'real,' hence less important, than the art itself. Plotinean art can be most moral by being most itself.

In this aesthetic there lies at least one knotty problem which will be of great importance in neoclassical, and in Cousin's, thought. How much does the artist contribute, and how much does nature itself contribute, to the creation of artistic beauty? The two components are interdependent, both depending on a transcendent source of all beauty. But how are they fused? A quotation will illustrate:

> Still the arts are not to be slighted on the ground that they create by imitation of natural objects, for, to begin with, these natural

objects are themselves imitations; then, we must recognize that they give no bare reproduction of the thing seen but go back to the Ideas from which Nature itself derives, and furthermore, that much of their work is all their own; they are holders of beauty, and add where nature is lacking. Thus Pheidias wrought the Zeus upon no model among things of sense but by apprehending what form Zeus must take if he chose to become manifest to sight.[30]

Plotinus endows the artist not only with the power to discover truth, but also to create it. Phidias evidently worked on a mental model, though no doubt also on an accumulated experience of the 'form' of matter, the form in which mortal eyes would know Zeus. This point is important, both as a kind of limiting case of Plotinus' aesthetic, one which shows his relation to later theory, and as a link in the present argument. Plotinus, who holds that both art and nature contribute to artistic beauty, is forced to consider the case of a Zeus, who is typical of those concepts for which no natural model can be found, and yet which must be realized in a natural medium. Normally, he argues, the artist directs his attention to the archetypal λόγοι, and tries to inspire himself by contemplating the spiritual power which made the forms of bodily beauty; he then experiences that inspiration together with the material object or situation to be represented. In such cases there is no suggestion that an 'ideal beauty' is invoked, but simply a profounder real beauty.

Plotinus' system is a spiritual monism, in which the ideal is most real, while the orthodox and neoclassical theory of 'ideal beauty' implies a spirit-body dualism between the 'ideal' and 'real.' In the case of the Zeus, however, where the only models available are themselves only interpretations, and nature enters only as the receptive medium to be formed, not as the inspiration, the creator must search in the *logoi*, i.e., in the depths of his fullest being, for something like a concept of Zeus. Here, perhaps, Plotinus comes closest to admitting something in the nature of an ideal beauty as it would be understood in neoclassical criticism. It is important to see that, even in this case, he does not conceive

30

the 'ideal' as a unified substance, but only as a perfection analogous to the reality to be created. Plotinus' other remarks on art must be understood in connection with this view of man's discovery of nature by going within himself. So, when he considers two stones, one of which has been sculptured while the other remains rough, Plotinus finds the superiority of the former solely in the art which sculptured it. He even says that art loses by being actualized:

> everything that reaches outwards is the less for it, strength less strong, heat less hot, every power less potent, and so beauty less beautiful.[31]

On the other hand, though nature seems to be only symbolic of some beauty which is its source, Plotinian nature itself is deeply formful and 'reasonable.' Like the nature in Schelling's aesthetic, it is, when fused with mind in art, a symbol of the actual rational structure of the world. Before that fusion it has its own reason, but at a lower degree of clarity, or form.

What I have called the Plotinian conspiracy between the artist and nature, for the creation of beauty, is faced as a basic problem by such a neoclassicist as Quatremère de Quincy, who adopts the terms of the problem in precisely its Plotinian form. Quincy, for example, wants to explain the superiority of artistic beauty to nature. He believes that the artist interprets nature in terms of an ideal model. The word 'ideal,' according to Quincy,

> applied to works of imitation, designates their characteristic quality, in as much as they are produced by the principle of the notions which belong to the labour of the judgment and understanding.[32]

Such 'ideal' imitation, in its contact with models in nature, copies

> the causes and motives of nature, in the formation of things and beings.[33]

The meaning of nature is essential to it, but can be discovered. There exists a harmony between the artist and nature such that the former can supplement the other's lack of form, or – in neoclassic language – of 'perfection.' To gain authority for his 'ideal' beauty, Quincy digresses on to a famous passage from Cicero's *Orator*, in which it is a question of the same Phidian Zeus which Plotinus discusses, and Cicero's interpretation of which Quincy wholly approves. Cicero holds that in that work Phidias had an ideal model in mind, not drawn from any particular object, and vaguely inspired by the sculptor's past experience, which consisted in discovering, in

> regard to the forms of bodies, a superior type of perfection, to the ideal example of which all objects presented to the eye are referred...[34]

His creation, though, was born out of his own mind;

> sed ipsius in mente insidebat species eximia quædam, quam intuens, in eaque defixus, ad ilius similitudinem artem manumque dirigebat[35].

This 'certain beautiful model' may or may not be applicable equally to a Zeus and to an Athena, which Cicero also speaks of Phidias' creating in such a manner. If it is not, Cicero's equation of this model with a Platonic idea will be unintelligible. If it is applicable to all creations of beauty, and this is probable, it is difficult to account for the necessary division of one ideal beauty into countless particular beauties. But Quincy's most revealing confusion is to associate this model of beauty – as Cicero had done – with a Platonic Idea. This is the identical error which Cousin makes in confusing Plato's notion of an ascending ontological scale of beauties toward the Idea of Beauty, with the 'ideal' beauty in the mind by which an artist or observer creates or appreciates 'real beauty.'

The answer to Quincy is that, as far as art is concerned, Plato never permitted the creator of it any access to those unchanging ideas as archetypes for his creation. Still this neoclassical error, put in its Plotinian form of an interpretation of the superiority of art to nature, preserves the essential direction which Plotinus

32

gave it. Quincy's position is typical of the neoclassical aesthetic, which created a metaphysical aesthetic without importing the whole metaphysical context in which the source, Plato or Plotinus, had conceived his thought. In a spiritual metaphysics like Plotinus' there is less need, for the purpose of describing the nonempirical contribution of the artistic creator, to introduce an ideal beauty; the full empirical expression of 'real' beauty is a profound means to the discovery of natural essence or form, and such realized form is the maximum that artistic beauty can offer. Since everything is instinct with form, nothing is as ideal as is the real, potentially.

This position does not save Plotinus from the need to explain, in more than structural terms, the contribution of the artist to his creation. So he awards the artist a deeper knowledge of the knowledge which is dormant in nature. But Quincy's nature is not so co-ordinated with spirit. He points out that nature is not only more imperfect than man's idealizing capacities, but it is not, to our point of view, seeking its own perfection; or if it is, its perfection is alien to our understanding. So finally, twisting the context of Plotinus, to whom he shows his basic inheritance in the matter of the Zeus, Quincy introduces the 'beau idéal,' wholly within the mind and not within nature, and in such a context inevitably smacking of the unreal. Quincy is only the last in a tradition of theorists under Plotinian influence; his most important predecessor, in exploring the problem of ideal beauty, having been Winckelmann.

Cousin is heir to much of Quincy's neoclassicism. Because of this indebtedness I have examined Quincy's position here; it introduces Cousin's debt to Plotinus. Cousin does not face the Plotinian artist-nature problem directly. He asserts, here reflecting indirect Plotinian influence, a superiority of artistic beauty over natural beauty. He writes:

> L'art est une nature perfectionnée qui conçoit l'unité sous la variété.... l'idéal sous le réel, et qui cherche à reproduire l'objet de cette conception, mais avec des formes qui lui soient moins

infidèles. L'art imite la nature, en ce sens qu'il lui dérobe l'idée morale ébauchée dans chaque objet; l'art surpasse la nature, en ce sens, qu'il rend les formes plus pures et mieux appropriées à l'idée morale qu'elles expriment.[36]

This superiority is intellectual, rational, not one of vitality. The basis of vitality is the diversity of nature, the 'real' without which art is pale. But the specific cause of art's greatness is the ideal beauty which the creator of art cognizes simultaneously with the real beauty in nature. Admittedly the real beauty in nature has an upward urge toward more spiritual beauties, which it symbolizes. Real beauty in all things is itself moral beauty. Cousin is here more Plotinian than Quincy, to whom, nevertheless, he probably owes his own formulation of the essential intelligence of nature. But in his 'beau-idéal' theory Cousin speaks from the heart of neoclassicism; though differing in details from Quincy's, Cousin's 'beau-idéal' is the perfection of the real, contingent, changeable beauty with which it is originally perceived. It is always more beautiful than the beauty perceived. The artist creates and the observer appreciates in terms of it. Its source is 'l'idée du beau,' which can present itself in the unique perfection of the particular beauty experienced, and that without depreciating its own substantial unity. Artistic creation, then, does not involve a progressive understanding, whereby an ideal beauty would be conceived simply as the experience-gained conception which is always richer than its realization. Rather Cousin explicitly confirms Quincy's interpretation of the 'ideal,' as a direct derivation from the Greek εἶδος; and he sanctions Quincy's use of Cicero's argument in the *Orator*, which clearly involved Cousin in the same problems that Quincy met. So Cousin attaches himself to the 18th century conception of the superiority of art to nature, a conception itself inherited from Plotinus.

I have not exhausted the importance of this particular Plotinian influence on Cousin. The vindication of art against Plato's attacks serves, logically, only as the ground for further aesthetic thinking. All of Cousin's thought which claims that 'l'art est lui même une sorte de religion' ultimately depends on Plotinus, and not, even had he known them better than he did, on the German idealists. This dependence holds for the association of beauty and goodness in art, and for the notion of a harmony binding artist or observer to artistic beauty: in Plato's thought, such claims for art are always condescending, because of his ontological depreciation of art. Cousin, however, can turn all these claims to art's advantage, and the aesthetic theorists who follow him will thus profit from ideas of which they hardly know the sources.

It is clear in what profound sense Plotinus can understand a harmony which draws the lover of beauty to a beautiful object or action. He adapts two basic notions of Plato here: that aesthetic experience is a kind of 'cognitive desire'; and that the object of such desire is a 'formed,' or fully 'existent' object of cognition, virtuous actions or studies thus being more beautiful than artistic beauty, which is finer than natural beauty. Love of beauty, therefore, is for Plotinus a spiritual union, the ground of which is a basic likeness in 'being' between the beautiful object and its lover. For Plato, this likeness did not exist on any level of being below beautiful human bodies, as he had no theory of symbolic beauty. And in the case of art, Plato only conceded to it a kind of simple and metaphorical, though potent, harmony with man's soul. In the monism of Plotinus, such metaphor is meaningless, because harmony can only be 'real.'

Such a vital notion of aesthetic experience leads Plotinus to a new interpretation of aesthetic judgment. This view has roots in the Greek mystery cults, which he knew, and which stressed purification as a preparation for union with the Absolute. Plotinus argues that the soul judges beauty only by stripping both itself and the perceived object of their material aspects. By this process light is brought into darkness, form into matter, being into non-being, and most important, goodness into evil (or non-goodness). As a result of this process, the beauty perceived can

35

be judged by the degree of spiritual harmony felt between the object and the lover of it. The degree of existence of the lover will regulate, as in Plato, the degree of existence of the objects which he can love. The highest beauty which anyone can love is the Ideas, the level from which the soul of man emanates. All souls yearn to be united to their source, which is the supreme Good, as well as the Beautiful. As Plotinus says:

> If a distinction is to be established among the intelligibles (The Ideas), we might say that intelligible beauty is the locus of ideas, and that the Good, which is located above the Beautiful, is its source and principle. If, however, we desire to locate the Good and the Beautiful within one single principle, we might regard this one principle first as Good, and only afterwards, as Beauty.[37]

On every lower level of aesthetic experience, also, beauty and goodness coexist. The major knot which Plotinus does not unravel is the one which resisted Plato in his analysis of how knowledge is possible. Man cannot appreciate greater beauties without being beautiful enough himself, and cannot become sufficiently beautiful except through the experiencing of higher beauty; so he seems condemned, though only logically, to the level of aesthetic sensibility at which he is born.

Plotinus explains more systematically than Plato the unity of goodness and beauty in aesthetic experience. Thus, while justifying artistic beauty, he canonizes the basically non-artistic nature of the Platonic aesthetic tradition. Neoclassical tradition, on the whole, imported the beauty-goodness union into artistic experience, while attending to the experience of beauty only in art. Cousin, who was more a philosopher than any of his neoclassical inspirers, knew directly his Platonic and Plotinian sources. He accepts the nonartistic context of beauty in the Platonic tradition, though holding to a chiefly artistic 'ideal beauty,' which hardly coheres with a view – originally Platonic – of the ascension through purely spiritual beauties. Now the moral harmony, which Cousin believes to bind the lover to the

36

beloved beauty, certainly has its original source in Plato, though neither the belief in the moral quality of nature, nor the explicit relating of beauty to goodness in aesthetic experience, is strictly Platonic.

The belief in the moral quality of nature is defended by Cousin in terms of a semi-Plotinian conception of the harmony of man with nature. He writes:

> Dieu, c'est le fond du vrai, du bien, et du beau; c'est l'absolu, qui se réfléchit tout entier dans toutes ses manifestations, ou, comme on dit ordinairement, dans toutes ses créations. Dieu est donc à la fois dans la nature et dans l'homme et c'est ainsi que s'explique la sympathie de l'homme pour la nature.[38]

As the first line shows, there is a Plotinian substructure here to what is probably an inspiration from German idealism. It will be clear later that Cousin's contested pantheism encouraged a Plotinian solution of the harmony felt in experiencing beauty. This 'sympathie' explains not only the harmony of man with nature, but the integration of beauty and goodness in all experiences involving the 'moi' with the 'non-moi.' In Plato this notion is clear, though never in the systematized form Plotinus gives it. Cousin attaches himself to the particular statement of Plotinus, that

> les hommes beaux sont seuls juges de la beauté.[39]

Beauty is moral, and man's degree of morality or purity is the measure of his aesthetic sensibility. As Cousin writes:

> le beau n'est qu'une beauté morale, une idée, un sentiment; il n'y a donc que l'homme beau, c'est à dire celui qui possède en lui, soit constamment, soit à un moment donné, l'idée ou le sentiment empreint dans la nature, qui puisse juger le beau, c'est à dire, retrouver dans le symbole extérieur, l'idée dont il est lui-même pénétré.[40]

or again:

> Toutes les fois que nous saisissons le beau à l'extérieur, c'est que nous le portons déjà dans notre esprit, c'est par notre côté moral

seul que nous pouvons nous mettre en rapport avec le moral de la nature.[41]

As suggested in the first line, this theory applies as well to all more spiritual beauties. It is tempting to press this influence of Plotinus even beyond harmony and the moral qualities of aesthetic experience. The Platonic aesthetic harmony rests on appropriate measures of man's soul, while Plotinus' rests on the mutual measures of the soul within and the soul without. On no other ground than a Plotinian aesthetic could the commensurable harmony of beautiful object and perceiver be defended. Much modern aesthetic thought records the advance and confusion caused by importing a faculty psychology into the experiencing of beauty, and associating special faculties with special aspects of the beautiful object, usually an art-object. Cousin clearly derived his own faculty terminology from Kant and Burke, but he may owe the source of this psychological practice to Plotinus' metaphysics. He probably owes to Plotinus the source of his cognitive theory of beauty, and thus the source of a notion which could readily be assimilated into the kind of harmony described here, between a faculty and an aspect of beauty.

Though Plotinus introduces his cognitive theory to explain the experience of art, especially as an answer to the Stoic theory of symmetry, it is so deeply rooted in his entire philosophy of being that it is equally applicable to all forms of beauty. The Stoics had held that beauty resides in the proper adjustment of parts in a single whole. Plotinus attacks the materiality of this theory, which concludes that beauty must be composed of parts, an idea hard to reconcile with belief in spiritual beauty.

> If material extension were in itself the ground of beauty, then the creating principle, being without extension, could not be beautiful: but beauty cannot be made to depend upon magnitude since, whether in a large object or a small, the one Idea equally moves and forms the mind by its inherent power.[42]

So Plotinus, with Plato, believes that some simple sounds, and simple colors, chiefly gold and other bright and light colors, are absolutely beautiful, as is spiritual beauty. On the other hand, most beauty has parts, but in strict subservience to a pervading unity. Plotinus contrasts his position to the Stoic position, writing:

> the wisdom of the artist... is not a wisdom consisting of manifold detail co-ordinated into a unity but rather a unity working out into detail.[43]

This unity, which proceeds from the intuition of divine reason when the mind contemplates nature, discovers, and expresses the form of nature; it follows that all the details of that expression have a homogeneity which cannot be explained if they are considered as correctly adjusted parts in a whole. Rather all the details have the kind of inalienable unity possessed by people educated as children in the same intellectual system. Thus 'unity in variety,' for Plotinus, is identical with 'being,' which is simply 'having form.' In this theory, the problem of ugliness is seriously raised for the first time in aesthetic. Plotinus says with Plato, and as Aquinas will say later, that ugliness is that which instantly repels the soul. Furthermore, ugliness is a lack of form or of being. But beyond this Plotinus hardly advances, and by finding that beautiful and base actions are the most evident examples of beauty and ugliness, he too gives in to the difficulties which the Platonic tradition must have in explaining art in detail. To be sure, he uses the concept of 'matter' to account for 'un-form,' but does not want to consider matter as existing. Inevitably he considers matter positively, and even defines the diminished being of the different lower emanated levels as being admixed with matter. But without any terms for aesthetic different from his metaphysical ones, he could hardly solve a technical problem like disvalue in art.

Cousin adopts the theory of unity in variety into his aesthetic, but without the context which made it such a profound, if imprecise, theory in Plotinus. The fact is that Cousin may owe this theory to Shaftesbury or Hutcheson: they, however, owe the idea to Plato and to the clarified Platonic statement in Plotinus. There is no doubt, either, that Cousin knew Plotinus' solution, which is the type of all later ones. Cousin himself thinks of unity and variety as

> deux éléments contraires et également nécessaires...[44]

rather than as entelechy and substance, as Plotinus sees them. Cousin's dualism, his 'spiritualism,' permits him to assume a fact which Plotinus denies, that the creation of beauty finds form through content rather than the reverse. This variation from Plotinus is associated, in Cousin, with a distinction: between the unity-variety nature of beauty, and the power of beauty for moral expressiveness, which I have shown Cousin accepting, along with Plotinus. For Plotinus, beauty's unity within variety is the moral expression of that beauty, is virtually the being of that beauty. But Cousin claims that:

> pour qu'un objet soit beau il doit exprimer une idée; présenter une unité qui fasse briller l'idée exprimée; être composé de parties différentes et déterminées; en d'autres termes, idée morale, unité et variété, telles sont les trois conditions du beau.[45]

To be sure, he adds quickly:

> L'élément le plus important de la beauté, c'est l'idée morale; l'unité et la variété doivent en être empreintes, et lui servir seulement de manifestation....[46]

Still, on this question any separation of the cognitive from the morally expressive aspects is a misunderstanding, not only of Plotinus, but of the Platonic tradition. Cousin further complicates his own position by introducing a close harmony between his faculty psychology, and the cognitive aspects of beauty just discussed. So he says:

> L'esprit doit offrir trois phénomènes correspondant à ces trois éléments: l'esprit doit saisir l'idée qui est renfermée dans l'objet,

40

apercevoir l'unité sous laquelle l'idée pure se réfléchit, et enfin les parties diverses dont cette unité est le lien. Le sentiment du beau, la raison et la faculté de représentation telles sont les trois conditions du goût[47].

The paradox here is that the groundwork for such subdivided theory is the Platonic, chiefly Plotinian, idea of the simple harmony involved in aesthetic experience, a harmony in which all the boundaries of faculties are merged in a single non-rational cognition.

This paradox is typical of the debt which Cousin owes to the Platonic tradition. That tradition, in antiquity, is concerned with art only as an aspect of beauty, and so explains art-experience in its widest relations with rational and moral experience. Though he defers to this great range of the tradition, Cousin is, more than he knows, in a tradition of art-critics or beauty-psychologists; men like Quincy, or even Shaftesbury, on the one hand, and Burke on the other. So in his cognitive, unity-in-variety theory, Cousin draws on the metaphysical solution of Plotinus, while evading the metaphysical problem of form and un-form altogether, and introducing a complex psychological interpretation. In his assumption of the ontological superiority of art to nature, he inherits Plotinus' familiar argument that art discovers latent profound form in nature. But because of neoclassical prejudice for the ideal in beauty, an ideal which Plotinus barely sanctioned, Cousin is prevented from establishing the art-nature relationship in a wider context in his philosophy. It should not be overlooked, though, that while he is little interested in nature, the rough affinity of his own metaphysic and its Plotinian-pantheistic assertions of God's presence in the world, with Plotinus' spiritual monism, opens to Cousin the theory of the experienced fusion of beauty and goodness throughout creation, and the consequent moral harmony between man and nature. Ravaisson was right: not only is Cousin's aesthetic one of the most brilliant parts of his philosophy, but the deepest part of his aesthetic is that in which

41

il cherche à établir que la beauté est une expression plus ou moins complète de la perfection spirituelle et morale.[48]

Though the roots of this idea are in Plato, it is Plotinus on whom Cousin mainly drew for it. It is an idea which, forming the basis of Cousin's theory of 'expression,' itself begets the 'art-pour-art' belief in the profound symbolic power of art, a belief which was to obviate any further theories of the 'beau-idéal,' at least in the neoclassic sense.

When Cousin is faced with Shaftesbury, the problem of distinguishing particular sources becomes harder. Shaftesbury is, in a sense, a modern fusion of Plato and Plotinus. He has made the thought of the Platonic tradition implicit in his own thought, so that the special debt of Cousin to him is hard to determine. In writing about Hutcheson's aesthetic, Cousin names Shaftesbury as a chief source of Hutcheson's thought. But following his usual practice, of not naming the sources of his own thought, he makes no further reference to Shaftesbury, in connection with aesthetic. There can, though, hardly be doubt that Cousin knew Shaftesbury, as he was widely read in 18th century English thought, and would be naturally drawn to the most Platonic mind since Plotinus.

Shaftesbury's metaphysic, like Cousin's, is in form built on the pattern of the individual. As the individual is a mind-directed whole, all of whose parts intersympathize, and work toward a common end, so is the universe a 'great whole,' with God for a regulating mind, and all the co-operating worlds and their parts as its body. This universe is a single, vital spirit of which everything partakes, and which directs every created thing's acts by a faultless order. What seems to the individual to be partial evil, is really total good, an act inscrutably directed by the world-spirit. Though the individual's accusation of the world as evil is set down as shortsighted, the analogy from his own person to the world-structure is rhapsodically justified. For this reason, self-inspection is of the utmost importance. In himself a person

42

finds those regulated parts and regulating mind which are the universe in miniature. His spirit he sees to be at once truth, beauty, and goodness. It is true because it is, beautiful because it is form, a unity in multiplicity, good because it moves in the rhythm of natural affection. As Shaftesbury puts it:

> what is beautiful is harmonious and proportionable; what is harmonious and proportionable is true; and what is at once both beautiful and true is of consequence agreeable and good.[49]

In this triple form, then, the universe exists. Shaftesbury is well aware of evil and ugliness, but refers them to lack of education, either as causing men to see evil where it is not, or to be evil when they are really not. To be themselves, both good and beautiful, men must develop freely in accordance with 'inner form,' the essence which is their significance in the universe. But less interested in abstract metaphysics than in aesthetic and morals, Shaftesbury elaborates on the nature of 'inner form,' with such clarity that he can be considered a 'classical moralist' as well as a new Plato.

The individual, or 'virtuoso,' develops his 'inner form' freely by allowing an unrestricted unfolding of his powers. His growth will be guided by the influence of good and beautiful harmonies from outside him, to which he responds with his whole being, in a tropism of (almost Platonic) 'cognitive desire.' This beautiful human will be an artist in all he does, or in all that proceeds from his form. He will create the purest beauty in his actions and thought. But he may be drawn to try to perfect nature after his own form.[50] Nature, though it could not be better than it is in the universe it is in, does not clearly express its form. A man who clarifies that expression is an artist: his recreation after his own form is, because of the oneness of the world-spirit in man and nature, simply a profounder discovery of essential nature. The artist creates after an inner plan worked out by his self-realization in conjunction with the striving form in nature.

The depth of harmony between nature and man can be illustrated by Shaftesbury's theory of literary genres. The harmony of nature-form, which is 'outer form' in art, with artist-form, which is the 'inner form' in a work of art, naturally determines itself to certain definite kinds of expression, i.e. the tragic, comic, epic, epigrammatic. So, in a typical case, it appears that though the genius, or free creator of art, must be above all original, this does not mean that Shaftesbury's real artist is freer of strict conditions in the nature of things than were the metaphysically defined artists of Plato and Plotinus. In fact, if Plato had believed more in the good determination of the artist-nature harmony, he would have been willing to grant to artists the 'original' freedom which he recognized they must exercise, to the danger of the state. Shaftesbury's optimism trusts in the necessary good of natural development, though he does waver constantly between pure optimism and an aristocratic desire for corrective aesthetic education. The 'virtuoso,' actually, is a man who has been educated, but only by the nourishment which his own soul chose freely. For Shaftesbury, every growth must be entirely interior.

Though Cousin enters into no details of the inner nature of the artist, he does inherit, whether chiefly from Kant or Shaftesbury, a theory of the genius.[51] The genius is a man who creates only by his own nature, and is free of any rules. He creates a work with no precedents. Such a concept is latent in Plotinus, in the freely determined harmony between the artist and his object, and of the artist himself with divine reason. Thus a spiritual monism grounds modern genius-theory, which may explain the absence of such theory from neoclassicism, in which a lack of confidence in real freedom is indicated by the presence of rules. Shaftesbury develops Plotinus' scheme into a modern form, in which the genius is thought to destroy nature in order to recreate it, and perfect it after his own 'inner form.' Cousin follows such thought, when he writes:

> Le génie est ce qu'il y a de plus éminent dans l'humanité, et le
> génie détruit la nature, tout en l'adorant; et après l'avoir ren-
> versée, il la rétablit plus pure, et plus conforme à l'idée morale,
> gravée en elle de la main de Dieu. [52]

The Plotinian framework of Cousin's statement indicates he may
well be adapting Shaftesbury's neo-Platonic notion of genius.
The faith in the moral idea in nature excludes, here, the direct
influence of Kant. Perhaps the freedom which Cousin demands
for art, from religious or moral ends, is partly supported by a
Shaftesburyan faith in the goodness of free artistic creation.
Cousin sanctions Plotinus' idea that the beautiful man alone is a
judge of beauty, and also a creator of beauty. No doubt Cousin
absorbed some of Shaftesbury's faith in free creation by a beautiful virtuoso. The Platonic tradition, which opened with attacks
on the inspired artist, such as Ion, in Shaftesbury rises to the
defense of the genius, in terms of the moral-aesthetic harmony of
man with nature.

Shaftesbury holds that the work of art bears the unique print
of the artist who created it. As the artist himself was a unity in
variety, a governing mind in a diversified organism, so the art-
work will be a one-in-many. The unity in the work will correspond
to the peculiar 'inner form' or 'interior numbers' of its creator.
Of course, this form will be also the true form of the matter made
into art. In the process of this creation, the artist must first
mediate the nature of his subject, and establish a full plan to
work by. The total conception which assumes being, provided the
artist is a free, beautiful man, will be instinct with beauty,
goodness and truth, all of which is best symbolized by unity-in-
variety. Because, in fact, unity-in-variety is identical with that
trinity:

> The same features which make deformity create disease. The same
> proportions which make beauty afford advantage. [53]

And the truth or being of the universe is the harmonious co-
functioning of all elements to one end.

Shaftesbury's notion of unity in variety is quite similar to Plotinus'; with the exception that, in Shaftesbury, the notion is more proper to an artistic cognitive theory, though it is applicable to all realms of beauty, of which Shaftesbury thinks the beauty of act and thought the finest. For Plotinus, the form which the artist, in the manner of God, imposes on his creation, is the only beautiful aspect of that creation. For Shaftesbury, of course, the multiplicities of beauty are a delight to the soul just as the various organisms which compose the great whole of the universe are esteemed for their 'sufficient perfections.' This is quickly obvious to any reader of the *Second Characters*. Shaftesbury's essay on the *Judgment of Hercules*, an inspiration for Lessing's *Laokoon*, is a precise (even 'nice') survey of the adjustment of the elements of a painting so they may conform to a single significance. In Shaftesbury the concept of unity in variety tends away from the form-matter interpretation to one of an Horatian decorum in which no parts are conspicuously outstanding in the whole. Thus Shaftesbury, in a different way from Plotinus, may contribute a special sense to Cousin's cognitive theory of unity in variety. Within the province of real beauty, Cousin stresses the delightfulness of the variety which is unified. He attributes the vitality of beauty chiefly to the various, contingent elements in it. He even says this of a mathematical proportion, the aesthetic pleasure of which derives from one's observing a long and careful deduction. In the case of artistic beauty, he holds that in the pure search for the essential unity of his subject, the artist would awaken no warm interest in his work. There is no need to assume that Cousin knew Shaftesbury's art-criticism, most of which has been published since Cousin's death, but it seems probable that either Shaftesbury or his semi-disciple Hutcheson led Cousin to stress that the beauty of unity is directly proportionate to the degree of variety.

Though Shaftesbury's theory of unity in variety seems more an artistic theory than its precedent in Plotinus, Shaftesbury makes much of the beauty diffused through all being. His belief, much like Plotinus', differs from that expressed by Plato in the *Symposium*, chiefly in his admission of a degree of beauty to nature. Throughout the *Moralists*, Shaftesbury praises Nature both for the constant evidence it gives of correct adaptation and final causes, and because it serves as a model for man's own life. Man's self-inspection will bring him back to his own 'nature' and enable him to find the corrective laws of his being. These are the laws of broad development of all one's faculties under the guidance of a constant spirit. If Nature is so meaningful in this way, it plainly contains some form which can make it accessible to human artistry. But, though exploitable, the beauty of nature is uncreative and inert. Similarly, the beauty which man can create or be is inexpressive compared with God's beauty. So Shaftesbury writes, of the three orders of beauty:

> first, the dead forms, (those of Nature), which have no forming power, no notion or intelligence. Next, the forms which form; that is which have intelligence, motion and operation. Thirdly, that order of beauty which forms not only such as we call mere forms, but even the forms which form. For we ourselves are notable architects in matter, and can show lifeless bodies brought into form, and fashioned by our own hands, but that which fashions even minds themselves contains in itself all the beauties fashioned by those minds, and is consequently the principle source, and fountain of all beauty.[54]

Elsewhere, Shaftesbury says that these 'dead forms' are the mere lines of the human body, or of natural objects; thus he reveals a certain neoclassical prejudice for equating essential beauty with outlines or geometrical patterns. This 'dead form' is 'outer form,' he holds, and whatever 'inner form' is in nature is simply a reflection from a higher level. Still, in Shaftesbury's new concept of the vital creative, or 'forming,' force as a measure of beauty, there hides a romantic theory which will not evaluate beauty in terms of the kind of object in which it appears. Shaftesbury's own ascension scale is a metaphysical survival, in aesthetic, which had been necessarily introduced for the notion of

47

'spiritual beauty,' but which was distinctly moderated in the bulk of Shaftesbury's thought, where he shows his profound sympathy with the meaningful form in nature. His difference from Plotinus in this matter can be described as that of a pantheism which tacitly confounds spirit with matter, from a spiritual monism, which struggles to ignore matter.

I mentioned earlier that Cousin directly accepts Plato's statement of the elevation to God through spiritual beauties, as it appears in the *Symposium*. Cousin also admits the beauty of nature into this scale. He says:

> La beauté physique, ou la beauté des formes et des mouvements, n'est qu'un reflet de la beauté morale et intellectuelle, que nous pouvons comprendre sous le seul terme de beauté spirituelle ou immatérielle.[55]

The moral aspect of all these beauties accounts for their unity and for the feeling of harmony which Cousin believes to hold between man and beauty. This feeling is the 'sentiment du beau,' which in practice Cousin usually refers solely to the experience of art. He defines it as a feeling midway between sense experience and rational judgment; plainly he is borrowing from Kant here. But outside the Platonic tradition, there is no precedent for the enthusiasm which is attributed to such a 'sentiment.' I have remarked that Cousin calls it

> un sentiment exquis d'amour pur et désintéressé,[56]

saying that it provides

> une joie douce et tranquille, une sorte d'épanouissement.[57]

The least acquaintance with Shaftesbury's *Moralists* would have shown Cousin a precedent for such emotions in the presence of any beauty. Just as Shaftesbury, the least metaphysical of the Platonists, finds vitality in directly sensed nature, so he also describes aesthetic emotion as a spontaneous sense - and mind-

48

delight which is more fully its own end than the uptending meta-physical-artistic experience which always concerns Plato. Still it is clear that Shaftesbury is describing a form of 'cognitive desire.'

Thus, like Plato, Shaftesbury conceives of the 'harmonized' individual's experience itself as a cognition of truth in the world around him. In terms of this experience, Shaftesbury believes, the individual builds up a complete picture of the universe, after the analogy of himself. That universe is instinct with harmonies, binding each individual to its genus, and each genus to the one above it. This inter-communication of all beings is the ground of aesthetic harmonies which readily obtain between two created things. Shaftesbury interfuses the beautiful and the moral more like the 19th century aesthete than like Plotinus, or even Plato. Shaftesbury will even argue that the cause of bodily illness is an appreciable disharmony, or ugliness of bodily parts. Cousin does not agree: for him even the morally good seems only secondarily beautiful. But he seems to recognize, in the case of the artistically beautiful, a harmony of 'enthusiasm.' With Shaftesbury, and also Plato, Cousin does hold that this harmony affects all created realms, physical, intellectual, and moral. But his chief emphasis is on harmony in the realm of art. His apology for art profits from a concept of harmony which originally, in Plato, had even an anti-artistic bias. So Cousin's notion of unity in variety, which is, in his philosophy, hardly applicable to any but artistic beauties, probably derives in part from Plotinus. I have shown, however, that Shaftesbury seems to contribute a new emphasis on the variety of beauty: it required a philosopher doubling as an art critic to point this out. Perhaps it is in his faith in the good-ness of the free development of the artist's faculties, that Shaftesbury most impresses Cousin. Later, when it is clear that the influence of German idealism was much weaker on Cousin than was Platonism, it may well seem that Shaftesbury's theory of genius was Cousin's model.

In Shaftesbury, then, an 'aesthetic attitude' is reached which is

49

the natural outcome of the Platonic aesthetic tradition. Both really and metaphorically that tradition is 'inwardly.' The inward nature of the world is presumed to be a harmony which pervades all existence. This harmony is not simply an external continuity, but an existing sympathy, relating some (in Plato) or all (in Plotinus and Shaftesbury) created things or their acts. In general, this harmony is equated with being, and, after the pattern of a spiritual monism, being is equated with goodness and beauty. It thus becomes possible to consider the experience of beauty as moral experience, and, in fact, as the only real experience. This argument, important in Plato, is justified for the case of art in Plotinus, and in Shaftesbury is transformed into a total conception of man's relation to the world. All growth, for Shaftesbury, is a conspiracy between inner and outer harmonies, On the analogy of inner and outer harmony, Shaftesbury creates his metaphysics.

From this 'inwardly' tradition Cousin drew the major inspiration for his aesthetic. The result is a mixture: doctrines assimilated from the Platonic tradition are expressed with the 'outwardliness' which characterizes Cousin's thought. But his 'outwardliness,' conspicuous here in a desire to establish a totally coherent system, is suited to the absorption of the Platonic tradition. Admittedly, by forcing his aesthetic into the frame of the 'théorie de la raison,' Cousin violates the qualitative descriptions of cognitive experience, by which Platonism attempts to explain the ascension to the highest spiritual beauty. But aside from his 'beau-idéal' concept, and, negatively, a much diminished emphasis on the act of knowing beauty, Cousin scarcely intrudes the machinery of the 'theorie de la raison' into his aesthetic. His innate Platonic idealism, furthermore, renders this tradition congenial to him in a way that German idealism never became. The obvious affinity of the 'théorie de la raison' with mystical Alexandrian ἔνωσις is only strengthened by Cousin's attacks on Plotinus' mysticism in *Du Vrai, Du Beau, et Du Bien*. There Cousin rapturously describes the very experiences he is descrying.

The Cousin who would finally urge that the only important motto is *Sursum Corda*, sympathized always with any thought which depreciated 'matter' to the advantage of spirit.

There are three main points at which the Platonic aesthetic considered in rough abstraction from its representatives, locates the harmony of beauty: in the scale of physical, intellectual, and moral beauty; in the individual, considered independently of the chain of ascending spiritual beauties; and in art. In Plato and Plotinus it is a transcendent fusion of the ideas of beauty and goodness which originally makes that fusion possible in experience. But in both thinkers the inherence of those fused Ideas in the nature of things affords an ethical and 'ideal' quality, to real aesthetic experience, which negates the concept of a 'beau idéal.' Thus beautiful bodies, natural forms, thoughts or deeds are loved *per se*, because they express a moral beauty, to which man is united through his own spiritual harmony. Everything which is beautiful excites a love for itself because it is really akin to the beautiful in its lover. The individual himself is beautiful. He is a harmony and he responds to all harmonies outside him. For the Platonic tradition, the aesthete must be primarily a lover. As Plato showed, real cognition involves possession of its object by the whole, desiring mind-self. Only in a state of harmony is such cognition possible. Plato's sensitivity to false harmonies made him disclaim much art as ugly: only simple and obviously proportioned art struck him as harmonious. Plotinus opened a broader view of artistic harmony, by freeing art from slavery to nature, and allowing that it found the deepest harmonies, or 'form' in nature. Shaftesbury, finally, though faithful to the sensuous complexities of art, recognized that in its forming of nature, and its symbolizing of the unity-in-variety of its creator, beautiful art is a wide and useful harmony. In the end, then, an imprecise stress on the term 'harmony,' to characterize the aesthetic of the Platonic tradition, seems justified by the radical use of that term in Plato, Plotinus, and Shaftesbury, who practically equate harmony with being. Pushed to the extreme, as Plotinus pushes it, 'harmony' becomes any vitally interconnected co-existence, whether between external moral beauty and the individual, between the individual and an art-work, between art-work and nature, or among any aspects within any of these three elements. Harmony, then, becomes the only possible condition of intelligibility. The greatest theoretical difficulty of this tradition is to explain ignorance concretely by defining what non-harmony is.

I have mentioned that Cousin creates a precise correspondence between particular faculties and particular aspects of an art-work. The problem of harmony and disharmony never troubled him greatly. In metaphysics, he fought to restore a simple knower-known relation between the 'moi' and the 'non-moi.' He employed his impersonal 'raison' as a ground for this knowledge of matter by spirit. Cousin never describes harmony from the inside, as a unique individual experience on which the widest ontological analogies can be built, as Shaftesbury puts it, or even as an indispensable basis of education, as Plato holds. Cousin fails ever to associate harmony closely with the peculiar Platonic form of 'cognitive desire.' Such non-conceptual knowledge is basic to Plotinus, with his ἕνωσις, as well as to Shaftesbury, with his knowledge through union of spiritual parts. Cousin was always afraid of the taint of mysticism, which his age easily found in any non-rational cognition. His solution was a 'raison' which is independent of man as subject, and so applicable to all men as equal in experience before God, but which also cognizes primitively in an immediate grasping of truth. So while solving, in a roughly Platonic (or Schellingean) manner, the problem of knowledge, Cousin carefully puts his 'théorie de la raison' under the sanction of concept-categories, which he reduces to cause and substance. Harmony as experience is here hardly made explicit for discussion. Still, a deep assumption of existent harmony underlies all that is important in Cousin's aesthetic, and I have shown some of the debts which he owes for this belief.

The close relation of the absolute Ideas of Beauty and Good, both transcendent and embodied in the created world, enabled him to hold that the rising scale of physical, intellectual, and moral beauties have a unity in their common moral expressiveness, and can thus stand in harmonious relation to man. This harmony is experienced in a delightful 'sentiment du beau.' But to experience this 'sentiment,' the individual must be beautiful himself, so that he is in concordance with the beauty outside him: the more spiritualized he is, the more spiritualized his experiences can be, and the higher harmonies he can respond to. Between man and morally beautiful art, similarly, a harmony holds. Each depends on the other's spiritual beauty. But the morality of an art- work stems only from inner unity, a harmony of parts within the whole, which cannot be created for any other purpose than the pure creation of beauty. Cousin crowns his defense of the spiritual quality of aesthetic experience by asserting the free, organic nature of art, which itself is a clarification and perfection of the harmony in nature. But it is only necessary to recall Cousin's 'beau idéal' theory to see his distance from conceiving the profundity of the 'really' beautiful in the same way as this tradition. From Cousin's neoclassical half-depreciation of nature we draw our conclusion: that he owes only a partial debt to Plotinus in the matter of asserting the superiority of art to nature. He affects to believe that by retreating as far as possible within himself the artist gets as close as possible to the essence of nature, but since he has abandoned the radical spiritual monism of Plotinus, he is left more with an abstraction than with an essence.

# IV

Cousin's own Platonic aesthetic shows the mark of neoclassical neo-Platonism. There is a special difficulty in finding the specific sources of this influence; many sources are possible, especially during the very popular polemic which raged about neoclassicism from 1800 until the time when Cousin lectured on *Du Beau* in 1818. Since the most obvious neoclassical predecessors of Cousin's aesthetic are Winckelmann and Quincy, I direct my attention to them. It will be clear that Cousin chiefly adapted ideas of theirs which could be harmonized with his own basic Platonism. I must, though, at least glance at Cousin's debts to Hutcheson, Reid, and Burke before going on to Winckelmann. In the two Scottish philosophers Cousin finds reasonable, at worst modified sensationalist, theories of beauty, which reflect the anti-sensualism of their philosophies. Cousin studies them with something like personal pride. He would hardly have taken such pride in Burke.

For my purpose, Cousin's two short critical studies on the Scots have special importance. They are the only explicit studies of other aesthetics which Cousin has left. Further, since both Scottish thinkers consider aesthetic in terms of epistemology, primarily, Cousin's studies offer an insight; into what stimulated his own views, especially of the autonomy of aesthetic experience. I pointed out the way Cousin adapts from the

Platonic tradition an equation of beauty with goodness; an equation which justifies faith in unimpeded aesthetic experience. But that tradition does not elaborate on the elements of the kind of autonomous experience by which beauty is known. Such study is hardly made systematic before Kant, though eighteenth century aesthetic marks a steady progress toward it. As theorists of such definition of aesthetic experience, Hutcheson and Reid are important for Cousin.[58]

He expounds the aesthetics both of Hutcheson and of Reid in his *Cours d'Histoire de la Philosophie moderne*, v. 4, 1846. With great clarity he points out the dependence of Hutcheson on Locke, and the resulting compromise of 'idealism' with sensationalism in Hutcheson's aesthetic. Cousin sees Hutcheson as the first modern aesthetician, though a disciple of Shaftesbury, and places his work at the head of many famous Scottish aesthetic works, of which he mentions those of Reid, Gerard, Campbell, Beattie, and Dugald Stewart; he enjoyed a full knowledge of one strain of eighteenth century aesthetic. Hutcheson's importance, Cousin sees, is to have isolated beauty as a unique object of experience, so to have opened the way for a final break from neoclassicism, a break which was completed by Kant.

For Hutcheson, beauty is immediately 'sensed' by a particular 'internal sense' which operates by reflection on, and in conjunction with, the data furnished at the same time by one of the five normal external senses. Though, in fact, these internal sensations vary among men, as originally received they are identical, and are modified by the associations of ideas which vary in all people. But in every case the sensation of beauty is disinterested, and sought independently of all advantage. It is also immediate, despite the fact that the interior sense of beauty, as of goodness, is described by Cousin as 'réfléchi.' In its immediacy this internal sense is, in all men, directed to the same external qualities, universally considered beautiful. Those qualities reduce to unity in variety, a theory which Cousin here mentions as going back to Plotinus. Hutcheson, like Shaftesbury, says that the order which is created by this unity-variety relation is the order of the universe in miniature, and that it is as evident in nature as in art. It is the mark of form, which, like Plotinus, Hutcheson sees as the proof of beauty.[59]

Thus Hutcheson rehearses some of the premises of idealistic aesthetic, without denying his premise of the sense origin of all experience. He is able to avoid, in this way, the frequent neo-classical confusion of aesthetic experience with discursive rational experience. The typical neoclassical statement, found in Crousaz or even in Dubos, holds that aesthetic cognition gives just the knowledge which reflective reason would have given, if it had had the chance to operate at length. Cousin sees the importance of Hutcheson's initial break with this view, which was popular not only in Batteux's time, but into the late stage of the neoclassicism which Quincy headed. But Hutcheson's error, Cousin maintains, is to have ignored the distinction between two kinds of 'raison.' Hutcheson confused all reason with a lengthy logical process, in his insistence that man could never have reasoned himself to an understanding of beauty. Cousin has his own 'théorie de la raison,' which he expounds here for the purpose of refuting Hutcheson, and casts in the form of a theory of aesthetic judgment, which he discusses at more lenght in his section *Du Beau*. He insists that no faculty of sense alone can account for aesthetic experience, but that such experience always includes a 'rational' judgment, which is unvarying among all men. The dictates of 'raison,' as we have seen, are impersonal, and so independent of the particular experiences or associations of the individual. But though unchangeable, those dictates are closely fused with the particular, contingent sense-experience from which they arise. Still, though Cousin recognizes more complex factors in aesthetic experience than does Hutcheson, he never interfuses them, and 'judgment' always remains an unassimilated, absolute faculty. Only in trying to propose a kind of knowledge which will have the immediacy of Hutcheson's sense knowledge, and the certainty of rational principles, is Cousin pushed to an improved solution, one

56

related to Kant's. In the same way, he is led by Hutcheson's attempt to establish the disinterestedness of the 'interior sense,' his sharp distinction of the beautiful from the sensually agreeable, to clarify his own notion of the selflessness of aesthetic experience.

Reid seems to Cousin to have marked a real progress over Hutcheson in the matter of aesthetic judgment. Reid believes that judgment is involved in all feelings of taste, and writes:

> When a man pronounces a poem or a palace to be beautiful, he affirms something of that poem or palace; and every affirmation or denial expresses judgment.[60]

The reason why this judgment is passed is that the beautiful, or grand, or novel object derives its quality from the imprint of the intelligence which created it. Reid continues:

> I apprehend, therefore, that it is in the moral and intellectual perfections of mind, and in its active powers that beauty originally dwells; and that from this, as the fountain, all the beauty which we perceive in the visible world is derived.[61]

Since, therefore, there is an intellectual quality to every beautiful object, the perceiving mind must pass an intelligible judgment on its object. Reid finds this judger-judged relation holding between man and a scale of beauties which ascend, in the manner described in the *Symposium*, from natural beauty up through more and more pure spiritual beauties, each of which bears the imprint of its creator's intelligence. Cousin approves of this theory with its notion of judgment grounded in a Platonic scale of spiritual beauties. It would be misleading, though, to stress the influence of Reid's aesthetic on Cousin, as that aesthetic is contained only in the brief eighth chapter of Reid's *Intellectual Powers of Man*. Cousin's praise of it is important for showing, if there is any doubt, just where his sympathies lie. He remarks elsewhere that he is pleased to have the support of Reid's theory for his own views on moral beauty.

Burke, whom Cousin refers to occasionally in his aesthetic,

contributes originally to the affective aesthetic by which the eighteenth century was gradually making its way toward Kant. Like Hutcheson, Burke proposes to investigate the origins of certain aesthetic feelings which he describes as those of the beautiful and of the sublime. In his study on the *Sublime and Beautiful*, he considers man an animal whose feelings usually precede his thinking, and because of the creator's providence are just as likely as thought to conform truthfully to their objects. Burke trusts to the similarity, in all men, of the organs by which taste and imagination operate; he finds this a guarantee of sufficient universality in aesthetic experiences. The universal feelings of pleasure and pain which accompany such experiences furnish Burke with the basis for his distinction of beauty from sublimity. In all painful and pleasant experiences, Burke attempts to delimit certain corresponding classes of objects, the sweet or sour, small or large, smooth or rough. Thus, even when he does not speak of the feeling of the sublime as the dissolution of bodily solids in the presence of a grand object, or of that of the beautiful as their pleasant stimulation in the presence of a smallish, compassable object, he tends to conceive all aesthetic experience materially. Cousin's real affinities put him far from such an aesthetic as this, for which the expression of the ideal through matter is pure fantasy, as is the fusion of beauty with goodness in art.

Yet since the difference of two such thinkers lies in their general emphases as much as in opposed dogmas, it is not surprising to find some traces of Burke's thought in Cousin's aesthetic. Cousin applies a complex faculty psychology to his aesthetic. He lists three components of taste: 'intuition sensible,' which is the faculty that represents the object perceived; reason, which perceives the essential unity of the beautiful object; and 'le jugement et le sentiment du beau,' the first of which discovers, while the other 'adores' the moral idea which is expressed in the unity and variety of the beautiful object. This analysis might be compared with Burke's definition of taste:

> On the whole, it appears to me that what is called taste, in its most
> general acceptation, is not a simple idea, but is partly made up of
> a perception of the primary pleasures of sense, of the secondary
> pleasures of the imagination, and of the conclusions of the reason-
> ing faculty, concerning the various relations of these, and concerning
> the human passions, manners, and actions.[62]

When one adds the primary premise of Burke's aesthetic, that

> beauty is that quality or those qualities in bodies, by which they
> cause love, or some passion similar to it,[63]

it is possible to find an exact correspondence in Burke for Cousin's
elements of taste. Burke's 'pleasures of the imagination' derive,
of course, from a special visual-aesthetic tradition, descending
from Addison and Akenside, which is foreign to Cousin. Likewise,
one sees instantly the difference of Burke's 'reasoning faculty'
from the 'raison' of Cousin, which operates by 'abstraction
immédiate.' It might be added that, as Mackensie shows in
*Critical Responsiveness*, later eighteenth century criticism dwells
on the juxtapositions of faculties as explanations of aesthetic experience. Nonetheless, there remains a similarity between
Cousin's definition of taste and Burke's; and it must at least be
explained as a reflection of the same psychological-affective
climate in aesthetic, which prevailed outside of neoclassicism
from the mid-eighteenth century on.

For the other two chief traces of Burke in Cousin's aesthetic,
I have less doubt about asserting genuine influence. Discussing
Reid, Cousin praises him for asserting the absolute distinction of
aesthetic experience from sensory pleasure. Through a confusion
of those terms, Cousin held, the eighteenth century was condemned to produce no major works of art. The deep anti-eudaemonism
of his own aesthetic (and ethic), which is rooted in the Platonic
tradition, makes him sensitive to the importance of Burke's
distinction between the sublime and the beautiful. Cousin does
not accept Burke's notion of the sublime as that which excites the
passion of self-preservation; no doubt because that explanation

59

tends to express the experience in physical terms. Cousin prefers to consider the passion one of admiration, as Reid did, rather than of terror. But Cousin holds, attaching himself to Burke's authority as well as to Kant's, that the sublime effects a moving unbalance in the emotions of its perceiver. Though Cousin's statement of this condition is couched, like Kant's, in terms of the disharmony of faculties, it rests on Burke's paradox of the 'delight' residing in the pain of the sublime. Cousin writes:

> mais le déplaisir que l'homme éprouve de la faiblesse de ses re-présentations est compensé par la jouissance que lui cause le triomphe de sa raison. C'est lorsque se produit cette dernière désharmonie que le beau est dit sublime, et c'est lorsque la raison et la représentation sont d'accord que l'objet conserve la qualification pure et simple de beauté. [64]

Beauty is, for Cousin, as for Burke, the object of spontaneous pleasure, though Cousin omits Burke's remarks about the gentle social pleasure which the experience of beauty produces.

Related to Burke's theory of sublimity was his notion of the surpassing emotional effects of poetry. Unlike the plastic arts, Burke held, poetry can hardly be considered imitative: it neither represents nor conjures up any clear images, so is better suited to strong than to clear expression. In his concluding section on words, he illustrates in detail the power which poetry acquires through vague and unanalysed connotations. He even implies a contradiction between artistic sublimity and real clarity. Cousin, praising this chapter of Burke's treatise, adopts Burke's notion of the 'puissance mystérieuse des mots,' while maintaining that the word is at once the clearest and the most 'vaste' artistic symbol. Cousin writes:

> Deux ou trois mots lui (the artist) suffisent pour exciter dans l'âme les émotions les plus profondes,

and

> Que d'idées, que de sentiments, réveille en nous le mot patrie; que de choses ne rappelle pas à l'esprit ce mot si bref et si immense;

60

Dieu! Qu'un peintre essaie de représenter Dieu ou la patrie, et
voyez s'il pourra produire des émotions aussi vives et aussi
profondes.[65]

This notion of the vague power of poetry serves for Cousin, as it
did for Burke, to support the belief that poetry is the supreme art.

What I have suggested as the possible influence of Burke on
Cousin must, as in the cases of Hutcheson and Reid, be taken only
as a sample; an indication of the importance of eighteenth century
affective theory as a source, often unrealized, of Cousin's aesthetic. As Cassirer says, it was out of a union of literary theory
with insistent systematic thought that the eighteenth century
created the science of aesthetic. In Kant that union realized
itself in a final conceptualizing of the limitations of art, and in
general of the experience of beauty. The defining of aesthetic
experience, in Kant's four 'moments,' attributed autonomy to it
as a unique combination of sense and rational experience into a
new experience. Hegel developed the latent conclusion in Kant,
as Schelling also had, by considering art an elevated and effective
mode of cognition. Thus the conclusions of German idealism
concerning art rejoin, in the context of organized philosophical
systems, the major premises of the Platonic aesthetic tradition.
For both traditions art is in some sense a revelation of the ideal
through the real. All idealist aesthetic reaches this conclusion
through a gradual definition of the experience of beauty. As
representing this defining tendency in eighteenth century aesthetic, then, the views of Hutcheson, Reid, and Burke have
their most general importance here. Each tries empirically to
explain the experience of beauty, by systematizing his feelings.
Cousin drew and accepted from them those explanations which
accorded with the Platonic idealistic structure of his aesthetic,
as well as with the German idealism, for which they had laid
foundations.

Cousin's debt to neoclassicism is likewise chiefly to a modified
form of Platonism.[66] But neoclassicism, as it appears in Winckelmann and Quincy, imported Platonism into its own original

context. Its most evident link with the Platonic tradition was its insistence that beauty is immaterial, and its description of an 'ideal beauty' which is related to the Platonic Idea of Beauty. On the other hand a neglect in describing the experience of beauty, and of the 'idealizing' aspect implicit in such experience, leads neoclassicism to describe supreme beauty as an abstraction. From this there follows a profoundly interwoven association of concepts, of beauty with purity, with the spiritual, with the linear, with the colorless, with the universal, with the moral. All that is intricate in beauty is, as R. D. Havens shows, depreciated by the reigning eighteenth century taste for simplicity.[67] This taste is greatly strengthened by the discoveries of Herculaneum and Pompei, and the resulting classical revival in the second half of the century. And it is pushed to enthusiastic expression in Winckelmann; quite the opposite of the refined Augustan expression of pleasure in the harmonious and balanced.

Like so many neoclassicists, Winckelmann was himself an art-critic, and lover of antiquity, rather than a philosopher. It is impossible to find in him the formal aesthetic discussions which stand out in Cousin's aesthetic. My attention will be directed to a pair of closely related beliefs of Winckelmann, which can be found in Cousin's notion of beauty. These are Winckelmann's understanding of 'ideal beauty,' and of the union of beauty and goodness. Winckelmann's 'ideal beauty' includes a number of the associated concepts which I mentioned above. That beauty, Winckelmann thought, descends to earth from a divine Idea of God. All human attempts to describe it are bound to fail, because it is too pure:

> We look upon beauty as a purest water drawn from the center of the spring; the less taste it has the higher it is esteemed because free from all impurities.[68]

Thus the purest beauty which man can create is, like Greek sculpture, that from which everything individual and grossly material has been eliminated, and which remains as an essential

62

unity and 'lack of determination' (Unbezeichnung). In practice, only line and surface can convey this true beauty. And the subject best able to receive such beauty is man, in whom the Idea of Beauty, which is spiritual, receives its fullest expression. Thus, standing in the full Platonic tradition, Winckelmann holds that the most beautiful portrayal of man at the same time expresses him at his most moral. It is worth remarking, since Winckelmann is the father of late neoclassicism in France, as well as the chief representative of the entire movement, that he bequeathed his neo-Platonism to his followers in essentially this confused form. His notion of the Idea of Beauty is undefined. Though it descends from God, who knows whether it infuses both man and nature, or is only conceived by man's mind? Bosanquet writes that Winckelmann's doctrine is based on

> the ancient notion that supreme beauty could only be attained by combining the partial beauties of nature.[69]

But when Winckelmann himself says that the artist

> must follow, not merely.... nature in its most striking and perfect appearances, in its most grand or agreeable forms.... but something still more transcendent and sublime.... that ideal beauty of which the model is not visible in external nature,[70]

he adds the recurrent interior pattern, or type, which may be considered either a product of experience or anterior to it, but is always more than the sum of the beauties in nature. In either event, artistic creation involves an archetypal beauty which must in some way be reconciled with the expression of the 'characteristic,' if aesthetic is to account for much great art.[71] Even Winckelmann's restriction of real beauty to the expression of 'eine edle Einfalt und eine stille Größe,' is applied to sculpture, the Laokoon or the Apollo Belvedere, which strikes us as 'characteristic' and 'expressive' by comparison with fifth century sculpture.[72]

Cousin's stated aquaintance with Winckelmann leaves no

doubt of his knowledge of Winckelmann's ideal beauty. Cousin's own discussion of ideal beauty turns chiefly on the way it is known, its component parts, and the faculties directed to them. But while Winckelmann ignores the problem of knowledge, he does express a passion for the ideal, and the related concepts which almost compose it; his passion resembles Cousin's fervor. The ideal, in Winckelmann's thought, is practically stripped of its doctrinal background, and equated with the noble and spiritual. He was one of the first critics to describe the immediate contact of the perceiver with the artist's moral individuality in aesthetic experience.[73] Cousin's own practical criticism, as in the chapter *De l'Art Français*, is of a similar moral-aesthetic kind, rapidly seizing on the 'spiritual' or 'ideal' traits of the work of art. Such moral-impressionistic criticism has roots both in Cousin's mentality and in his explicit relation to the Platonic doctrine of the fusion of beauty with goodness. But it is worth pointing out the special praise which Cousin lavishes on Winckelmann's description of the Apollo Belvedere. He quotes and interprets two separate passages from Winckelmann, and concludes

> pesez bien chaque mot de Winckelmann: vous y trouverez une impression morale. Le ton du savant antiquaire s'élève peu à peu jusqu'à l'enthousiasme, et son analyse devient un hymne à la beauté spirituelle.[74]

Cousin continues, furnishing his own illustrations of the beauty of an ordinary ugly person when performing an heroic moral act. Like the language of Winckelmann, too, Cousin's fortifies its spiritualistic argument with a cumulative, emotive motion, almost literally 'a hymn to spiritual beauty.' He realizes enthusiastically that logical bond of ideal beauty with moral expression which is one of Winckelmann's genuine links with the Platonic tradition.

The profound difficulties inherent to Winckelmann's doctrine are left for later neoclassicists, among whom Quincy struggled longest and most systematically to create a coherent aesthetic.

64

Quincy, unfortunately, lacked just the poetry of spirit which was too prominent in Winckelmann. But it cannot be denied that Quincy makes a grand effort to render art rationally intelligible. Where Winckelmann describes particular aesthetic experiences, Quincy generalizes from all aesthetic experience, and expresses himself in terms of a law. I have said something about Quincy's view of nature and of an interior model of beauty. Like all neoclassicists, he will accept only 'la belle nature,' not nature in its unordered richness. Though he makes it clear that nature's purposes and perfections are not man's, he admits a humanistic nature as an object for art:

> Imiter la nature, c'est étudier l'homme dans les lois de l'espèce humaine. Imiter ce qu'on appelle un modèle (a particular non-rationalized object in nature), c'est n'étudier souvent la nature que dans quelqu'une de ses nombreuses exceptions.[75]

The running battle which consumed Quincy's life of thought was aimed against the 'école du modèle,' which insisted that the imitation of real objects in nature was the best method for creating beauty. His basic objection was that this kind of art could not mean anything. Only the ideal, i.e., the 'intelligible,' could make beauty in art, and it could only be imprinted by man's mind. Quincy is unclear just how the mind contributes its ideality to the work of art. At one extreme he seems to believe in a Platonic Idea in the artist's mind, by which he intuits the perfection of the real object before him; or again Quincy will describe the experience of the artist as the choosing of certain forms in nature, on the basis of previous experience, and reuniting them in the creation of a new composite. Even in this latter case, the real particulars are confronted with some kind of interior model. Quincy's (like Reynolds') central belief is that 'la belle nature' respects only the species or type (as 'l'espèce humaine'); by studying the generalized, non-individual characteristics of which the artist simultaneously intuits the perfection unique to that particular species.[76] In any case, the 'idéal' which is achieved is not to be confused exclusively with the 'beau idéal,' as there exists an ideal ugliness, or an ideal oldness.... As Quincy says, of the 'idéal':

> un satyré peut l'être comme Vénus, la vieillesse et la laideur l'être aussi bien que la beauté d'Apollon.[77]

Quincy's ideal beauty, then, is a clarification of a real beauty, which is in turn a generalization from certain other examples of its species. Despite its unclarities, his theory of ideal imitation, with its metaphysical interpretations of mind and nature is a thorough effort to illuminate with reason (or 'idea') every dark corner of aesthetic experience. To confirm this with another example, look at the remarks on allegory in *De l'Imitation* (1823). Quincy admires allegory as a means of importing concepts into art. He admires the personification of famous people as deities who represent an appropriate virtue. René Schneider has pointed out the influence of Quincy in having allegorical figures placed as adornments on important buildings constructed during the early revolutionary period. This is Quincy's most explicit neoclassicism.

Any discussion of Cousin's relation to Quincy must be prefaced by a remark on dates. Quincy's first aesthetic appears in his *De l'Idéal* (1805), and contains his writings in the polemic with Eméric David,[78] which were later republished (in 1837) along with other of Quincy's writings. It is this work to which Cousin refers in *Du Beau* as containing the rich doctrine of the 'beau idéal.' There is little doubt that Cousin's deep interest in ideal beauty was inspired by Quincy, though it is true that Cousin interpreted even Plato's aesthetic idealism in the direction of a 'beau idéal' theory. It is argued by Schneider, though, that in Quincy's fullest expression of his aesthetic, in *De l'Imitation*, the influence of Cousin is apparent. The two men knew each other, and Quincy doubtless knew the 1818 lectures on *Du Vrai, Du Beau, et Du Bien*. It is not impossible that Quincy owes to Cousin the form of two main tenets pointed up by Schneider, that of the

66

archetype of beauty toward which ideal imitation tends, and that of beauty as moral expression of the ideal in the real, particularly in the human figure. The first tenet is expressed by Quincy in such a passage as:

> le but de l'imitation c'est d'atteindre au Type ou plutôt l'Arché-type, seul vrai, seul éternel, seul universel....[79]

Such a vague sentiment, which is doctrinally lost in Quincy's indefinite idealism, is not prominent in his thought, or remarkable enough to call for special notice. The same is true of his statement of the moral expressiveness of beauty: he restricts this quality to the human figure, and explicitly denies moral depth to the richness of nature, which the more Plotinian Cousin will admire. All that is typical of Quincy's 'système idéal' is present in his 1805 polemic with David, in the same form as in all his later work. I have no interest in denying the influence of Cousin on Quincy, but it is well to see that the latter, by no means an eclectic, could only adapt foreign thoughts which were already latent in the aesthetic which, to judge from his official actions and writings, he had formed by the first decade after the Revolution.

Cousin's thought, just because of his frequent modifications, was open to constant influence. Leading an active life through the first thirty years of the 19th century, he met neoclassicism as a living, much discussed force. Its influence enters his thinking almost unconsciously, and is, as appeared in the discussion of his Platonism, mixed with a substructure of that Platonism into a general idealistic theory. Thus Quincy's ideal beauty, which Cousin admires as the true cause of the creation of beauty, becomes confused with Plato's Idea of Beauty. The 'théorie de la raison,' which is invoked by Cousin from his first to his last writings to explain the ascension to ideal beauty, is at the same time falsely compared with the ascension through spiritual beauties which Plato describes in the *Symposium*. Actually that 'théorie' was probably adopted by Cousin from Schelling; and so it has its immediate roots elsewhere than in either Platonism or neoclassicism. In the same way, Quincy's notion of 'la belle nature' enters Cousin's aesthetic in a modified context. At one time Cousin proposes only 'la belle nature' as the proper object of art:

> Tout objet naturel, si beau qu'il soit, est défectueux par quelque côté. Tout ce qui est reél est imparfait. Ici, l'horrible et le hideux s'unissent au sublime; là, l'élégance et la grâce sont séparées de la grandeur et de la force. Les traits de la beauté sont épars et divisés. Les réunir arbitrairement, emprunter à tel visage une bouche, à tel autre des yeux, sans une règle qui préside à ce choix et dirige ces emprunts, c'est composer des monstres; admettre une règle, c'est admettre déjà un idéal différent de tous les individus. C'est cet idéal que le véritable artiste se forme en étudiant la nature.[80]

This approaches the 'norm' argument of Quincy.

At the same time, though, Cousin holds that everything in nature is eloquent, expressive, or symbolic of underlying moral truth. To each object in nature, in its individual participation in a 'great chain of being,' he attributes beauty. Though this is not the beauty of a representation in art, which alone Quincy considers, it is clear even from Cousin's practical art-criticism that he admires that nature itself. Again, though, it cannot be claimed that Cousin harmonizes his conception of beauties in the real world with those in the ideal world of art and aesthetic experience: this is his penalty for mixing Platonism and neo-classicism. There is no doubt, finally, that no matter how Cousin interprets nature, he believes that Quincy understates the importance of the real. In his eclectic manner, Cousin deplores the pure 'ideal' as much as the pure 'real.' He says often that the vitality of art springs from its resemblance to the complex, the 'variété' in nature. So:

> Il n'y pas d'idéal vrai sans forme déterminée,
> il n'y a pas d'unité sans variété, de genre sans individus....[81]

and numerous repetitions of the same thought.

68

If, then, Cousin seems only to draw Quincy's neoclassicism into his own theory where it can be harmonized or at least juxtaposed with a basic eclectic Platonism, it does not follow that Cousin escapes the problems which accompany Quincy's 'ideal.' Like Quincy, he accepts the 'ideal' as a knowledge-giving object of aesthetic experience, and so as the justification of such experience. He does put the 'ideal' in a clearer context than Quincy, making it the object of judgment, attained by 'abstraction immédiate,' and with its being on the level of the absolute idea of the 'beau,' which has a clearly defined position in Cousin's metaphysics. But he never determines whether the ideal is basically one or many, how it is related to the unity and variety of beauty, whether the ideal for different arts might vary.... In the same way, he involves himself in difficulty when he undertakes to consider the ideal non-metaphysically. With Quincy, and all neoclassicism before him, Cousin asks:

> Des tableaux d'un coloris médiocre.... ne nous émeuvent-ils pas plus profondément que telles œuvres éblouissantes, plus séduisantes aux yeux, moins touchantes à l'âme? [82]

He says too little on this matter to prove that he fully accepts the relation, in painting, of the linear and the pale with the ideal; but there is other evidence that he disassociates the 'ideal' from the values of the 'real.' So, after having claimed that imagination is the sovereign quality in an artistic genius, he goes on to say:

> Le propre des hommes d'imagination est de se représenter les choses et les hommes différemment de ce qu'ils sont, et de se passionner pour ces images fantastiques. [83]

Here artistic vision presents not the profounder vision of reality, which even the imitation of 'belle nature' reaches, but an escape world. In another place, discussing the moral quality of 'ideal' art, Cousin seems to be taking the word 'ideal' in a vulgar meaning of 'improving' or 'purifying morally.' Thus he believes that, in drama

C'est la nature humaine qu'il s'agit de représenter à elle-même sous un jour magique qui ne la défigure point et qui l'agrandisse. Cette magie, c'est le génie même de l'art. Il nous enlève aux misères qui nous assiègent, et nous transporte en des régions où nous nous retrouvons encore, car nous ne voulons jamais nous perdre de vue, mais où nous nous retrouvons transformés à notre avantage, où toutes les imperfections de la réalité ont fait place à une certaine perfection, où le langage que l'on parle est plus égal et plus relevé, où les personnages sont plus beaux, où même la laideur n'est point admise....[84]

I quote at length, as in this case Cousin's 'souffle' illustrates his thought. Cousin is transporting the Quincyan aesthetic sanction of the 'beau idéal' into the moral-aesthetic realm, a transfer which he justifies on the authority of the Platonic tradition. On this undoctrinal level, he achieves a kind of emotional amalgamation of the two traditions.

I conclude that Cousin's relation to neoclassicism is superposed on his deeper Platonism. Earlier I discussed Cousin's relation to Quincy's 'beau idéal,' in order to point up the different premises underlying the Plotinian and Cousinian views of the relation of art to nature. I concluded that the absence of a spiritual monism in the neoclassic tradition had, in a sense, put art in the position of artifice. Cousin's 'ideal' seems to share, with Quincy's, as with Winckelmann's and the rest of neoclassicism, this unreal tinge, and for the same reason that Quincy does. On the whole, though, by absorbing neoclassicism simply into an 'idealistic' aesthetic, with a spiritualistic, metaphysical cast, Cousin integrates the spirit of that doctrine into his own aesthetic. Thus, in different ways, he is able to accept the 'ideal' simply as that 'more than real,' and therefore intelligible, pure, and noble quality, which as a Platonic idealist he naturally admires.

# V

Study of Cousin's relation to German idealist aesthetic soon shows the meaning of his remark that he intended to import into France only so much of that new philosophy as would be easily absorbed. His grand aim is to nourish 'une philosophie française' along spiritualistic lines. To this end, he renders German idealism in pellucid, and accessible form, all involved with his own idealism. A reader of *Du Beau* is struck with how Cousin weaves the German elements into the native Platonic context: so the Hegelian 'division des arts' is authorized by a theory of aesthetic 'expression' which is rooted in Platonism; or the Kantian proof of the disinterestedness of aesthetic experience is placed in the frame of the *Hippias Major* argument, by which Cousin refutes false theories of that experience.

This is not to say that Cousin needed to distort his own or German idealism in order to harmonize them. Rather he drew on 'idealistic' elements, in Kant and Hegel, which could be disassociated from the particular, doctrinal schemes of their philosophies. True to an inner sense of universal, if superficially described, truths, Cousin shows by his synthesis the deep affinities of all idealist aesthetics. This affinity has been pointed out by Basch, in a study 'Des Origines et des Fondements de l'Esthétique de Hegel.' He writes:

L'esthétique de Hegel clôt en quelque sorte un mouvement qui remonte non seulement à Schelling à Schiller et à Kant, mais à Platon et à Plotin. Tous les grands métaphysiciens qui ont abordé le problème du Beau ont été amenés à considérer la sphère de l'esthétique comme une sphère intermédiaire, comme un organe de réconciliation, comme une harmonisation.[85]

Aesthetic studies experience which falls between rational and sense experience, which makes the realm of nature intelligible to that of spirit. I remarked, in discussing Hutcheson and Burke, the way in which they lead toward the defining of aesthetic experience in Kant's *Critique of Judgment*. Hutcheson's 'interior sense' is typical of the pre-Kantian description. Kant, in his *Critique*, attempts to place this experience between the realms which concern, respectively, reason and nature, thus to create a bridge between his first two *Critiques*. In so doing, he prepared a theory of the fusion of beauty and goodness: this same fusion is basic to the Platonic tradition, is in fact its manner of describing the cognition of beauty. True, Kant limits the beautiful to a mere 'symbol' of the morally good, but in his very proclamation of the autonomy of aesthetic experience, he justifies the belief that it can be independent of any moral evaluations, and can hence include its own morality. Hegel stresses the total freedom of beauty in art, and supports this stress by the belief that the work of art is a profound expression of the Idea in sensuous form. Hegel claims even more; that he has broken through the still unreconciled extremes of Kantian philosophy, subject and object, reason and nature (in its ultimate reality), in order to see, in art, the Idea's coming to consciousness of its existence in nature. Thus he sees in aesthetic experience that insight into the structure of the world which is reminiscent of the Platonic idealist aesthetic, with its belief in corresponding harmonies. It is only nominal that Hegel does not also describe this insight as a simple fusion of goodness with beauty.

So German idealist aesthetic, of which the extreme appears in Schelling, attains a position comparable to a Plotinian spiritual

72

monism. Though this eminent progress of German aesthetic is marked by its profound consciousness of the chasm to be bridged between man and nature, its subsequent description of the spiritual autonomy of aesthetic experience most closely relates it to the Platonic tradition. For that tradition expresses the intermediacy of beauty between man and nature, and does so in terms of non-conceptual, non-sensible 'cognitive desire,' by which the beautiful and good are fused. By this cognition the multiple was made to release the intelligible within it. Faith in the goodness of a harmonic experience of beauty led a late Platonist like Shaftesbury to a modern aesthetic world-view.

It is not surprising, then, that the nineteenth century 'aestheticism' of French theory should owe a demonstrable debt to Kant. For he and his successors, by proclaiming that beauty (or art) was an end in itself, declared the self-sufficiency of aesthetic experience as human activity. In Hegel, where the metaphysical context for aesthetic is the most elaborate, the resulting elevation of aesthetic autonomy is the most definite.[86] But it is not so much in the structure of their metaphysics that the Platonic and German idealisms are to be compared even here. It is in their common assertion of the value of free aesthetic experience, as a cognitive and moral experience, that the two traditions show their closeness. The Platonic 'cognitive desire' is simply a description of the kind of cognition which Kant defines in terms of subjective judgment. In this sense, most clearly, both traditions consider aesthetic 'comme un organe de réconciliation,' a union of the sensible (nature) with the intelligible (reason). Considered on this abstract level, the type of the neoclassical aesthetic brings the other two into relief. Neoclassicism depreciates the 'natural' far more than do the others, because it sees it as unintelligible, and in need of clarity, which is an abstraction from, and an essence of it. Thus neoclassical idealism frees itself from the contingencies of experience, while the two idealist traditions construct their aesthetic on the deep particulars of experience. Neoclassicism errs simply in the kind of

73

intelligibility it wants to assign to aesthetic experience, but not in its insistence that beauty is an object of knowledge.

The developing argument is that Cousin's aesthetic, being basically Platonic, accepted only influences which could be harmonized with that basis: we must first see whether Cousin adopted Kant's notion of aesthetic autonomy. It is known that Cousin was a pioneer in introducing Kant into France, and although the *Kritk der Urteilskraft* is the one major Kantian work which Cousin does not discuss, his detailed knowledge of the others, added to his references to Kant's ideas on beauty, authorizes an assumption that he had a thorough knowledge of Kant's aesthetic. There is evidence of Cousin's knowledge of the four 'moments' of the Kantian aesthetic: he insists on the subjective disinterestedness and subjective universality of aesthetic judgment. Cousin says:

> Le sentiment réveillé par ce jugement est tout-à-fait désintéressé, et, à un certain degré d'énergie, il peut prendre le nom d'amour pur, parce qu'il ne tend jamais à la possession de son objet.[87]

This thought is often repeated, and defended by a refutation of false theories of aesthetic judgment. Cousin disposes of the pragmatic, religious, moral, and personal interest theories, after the fashion of Socrates in the *Hippias Major*. Though he seems indebted to Hegel for his strongest statement of aesthetic freedom, there is no mistaking the influence of Kant's first 'moment' in Cousin's plainest statement of his 'art pour art' aesthetic. By argument from the pure self-adequacy of the 'sentiment du beau,' he concludes that art can only attain perfection through unhampered freedom:

> Le beau excite un sentiment interne, distinct, spécial, qui ne relève que de lui-même; l'art n'est pas plus au service de la religion et de la morale qu'au service de l'agréable et de l'utile; l'art n'est pas un instrument, il est sa propre fin à lui-même,[88]

and:

> Il faut de la religion pour la religion, de la morale pour la morale, comme de l'art pour l'art.[89]

But Cousin also makes much of the Kantian distinction between the passing of a relative subjective judgment, and a judgment of beauty which, in subjective terms, demands universal assent. Judgments of taste, Cousin agrees, involve only relative values:

> Si une personne me dit, en présence de l'Apollon du Belvédère, qu'elle n'éprouve rien de plus agréable qu'en présence de toute autre statue, que celle-là ne lui plaît pas, et qu'elle n'en sent pas la beauté, je ne puis contester son impression....[90]

But a judgment of beauty involves absolutes:

> Mais si cette personne conclut de là que l'Apollon n'est pas beau, je la contredis hautement, et je prononce qu'elle se trompe.[91]

It should be remarked that, in his aesthetic as in his metaphysic, Cousin contradicts Kant's subjectivism. He justifies his argument against the dangers of a relativist doctrine of judgment, by asserting that it would no longer be possible to consider this or that object as absolutely beautiful or ugly:

> il n'y aura ni beau ni laid, et la Vénus Hottentote égalera la Vénus de Médicis.[92]

Invoking his 'théorie de la raison,' he is able to insist that beauty in things is known as such and in the same way by all men, as an objective law. Thus Cousin accepts Kant's subjective universality, while adding his own notion of objective universality.

His view of the faculties which contribute to aesthetic experience seems a strange amalgamation of Kant (and perhaps Burke) with his own philosophy. Cousin is careful to distinguish between mere sense-experience, which involves desire, and the Kantian 'sentiment du beau,' which is pure. He declares that 'sentiment' is immediately experienced, as opposed, at any rate, to the 'utile': he may reflect Kant's insistence that aesthetic judgment involves no idea of the perfection of the beautiful object. On the other hand, he makes that 'sentiment' derive from an absolute judgment of beauty, which is infallible:

> Ce jugement aperçoit le beau, mais il ne le constitue pas; le beau n'est renfermé ni dans la matière ni dans l'esprit; c'est, comme nous l'avons dit, une des formes de l'infini qui nous est révélée à propos du visible, mais qui est elle-même invisible.[93]

The same difficult combination of reason with a 'sentiment du beau' appears in Cousin's theory of imagination. The basic element of imagination is a 'mémoire représentative,' from which 'volonté' makes certain abstractions, to which the 'sentiment du beau' (or 'amour') emotionally attaches the 'imaginer,' and the beauty of which 'raison' certifies. Thus, imagination is only the association of sentiment with the faculties of the mind (esprit): it is love united to memory, will, and reason. It is no longer even Kant's 'sentiment du beau' which is relevant, but the simple contrast between his imagination (the *à priori* faculty of intuition) and that of Cousin. In his *Préface* to the *Fragments Philosophiques* of 1826, Cousin described the 'moi' as existing on three planes: 'sensibilité,' 'volonté,' and 'raison.' This shows the characteristic and unspecifically 'aesthetic quality' of Cousin's description of imaginative aesthetic experience. Intuition, except in the guises of 'raison' or of 'amour,' is excluded from it. 'Volonté' is presumed to abstract and recombine its memory images. What real distinction is possible there between the action of 'volonté' and 'raison,' and what between those of the 'sentiment du beau' and 'volonté'?

Cousin agrees with Kant in his interpretation of the co-operation of these faculties in the experience of the sublime and the beautiful. He believes these two 'genres de beauté' to be distinguishable by the relations of 'sensibilité physique' to 'raison' in the experience of them. The harmony of these faculties produces the feeling of beauty, and the disharmony produces a feeling of sublimity.

> D'un côté se trouve le beau, de l'autre le sublime; d'un côté l'émotion douce, agréable, le bonheur; de l'autre un mélange de plaisir et de peine, une victoire et une défaite, un état complexe, enfin, qui est à la fois jouissance et souffrance.[94]

He dislikes Burke's definition of the sublime as the 'terrible' which excites the feeling of self-preservation, and turns rather to this Kantian description of the subjective determination of the two states. It is typical of Cousin to give a moral (and patriotic) example of his distinction.

> Je vous demande si l'esclave qui pleure paisiblement son esclavage et le héros qui donne son sang pour sa patrie, produisent sur vous la même impression? Êtes-vous ému de la même manière lorsqu'un homme ouvre sa bourse à l'indigent, ou lorsqu'il donne l'hospitalité à son propre ennemi et le renvoie comblé de présents? [95]

By passing to the moral sphere Cousin is enabled to avoid a problem of Kant's sublime, namely how reason is to grasp its object, if the senses are confounded. The other comparisons suggested by Cousin, as that of an ode of Horace to an Indian epic, or of Condillac to Aristotle, hardly make his point clearer.

Just as he adapted the Kantian definition of aesthetic experience to the purposes of his own idealism, so he takes the sublime-beautiful distinction as an occasion to praise the infinite reaches of reason, which, for instance, exceeds the senses in order to postulate an absolute space, pre-existent before created objects. Just as Cousin considers the free play of faculties the means of experiencing sublimity or beauty, so he adapts something of Kant's notion of the freely creating artistic genius. Kant, in saying that the genius gives the rule to art, through nature, stressed the native originality of such a creator. Cousin stresses a particular facet of that originality, its ability to destroy and then to recreate nature more perfectly after its own ideal. Artistic creation is neither an aspect of a 'science' or of a 'métier,' he asserts:

> La science connaît et l'art produit; l'art s'abjure lui-même, s'il se contente des théories; il perd de son éclat, quand il veut devenir une pure philosophie....[96]

Cousin says little enough on this matter; we cannot be sure about his relative debts to Shaftesbury or to Kant. It is more important to see this as another element of his aesthetic which is adapted to the purpose of showing the spiritual superiority of artistic beauty and of man to nature.

The question of his relation to Hegel's aesthetic is complicated by a matter of chronology. Cousin's 1818 *Cours*, delivered immediately after his trip to Germany, was not published until 1836, at which time he had abandoned much of his Hegelianism, and probably deleted some from the text. Further, Hegel's *Vorlesungen über Ästhetik* were unpublished until 1835, though the substance of them was well known before that. It is likely that Cousin picked up aesthetic views from Hegel when he visited him in 1817; as Kuno Fischer remarks, Hegel gave his first aesthetic lectures in 1817-18.[97] The decisive factor, perhaps, is the real agreement between three Hegelian notions and their equivalent in Cousin: the notion of the absolute freedom of art; that of beauty as an 'expression' of the Idea in sensuous form; and a hierarchy of the arts, deriving from the expression theory.

Hegel's doctrine of the freedom of beauty is based on Kant's proof of the autonomy of aesthetic experience.

> Ohne den Zustand der Freiheit von Seiten der subjektiven Betrachtung gibt es keine ästhetische Welt. Ohne diesen Zustand ist nichts ästhetisch: diesen Zustand vorausgesetzt, ist alles ästhetisch.

And so,

> ist die Betrachtung des Schönen liberaler Art, ein Gewahrenlassen der Gegenstände als in sich freier und unendlicher, kein Besitzenwollen und Benützen derselben als nützlich zu endlichen Bedürfnissen und Absichten.[98]

But this freedom of beauty, in art especially, is justified by Hegel as more than a necessary condition of aesthetic experience. He claims that in artistic beauty the Idea, by being embodied in sensuous form, comes to selfconsciousness of its own past in unconscious nature. Thus art is the first of three stages of the self-consciousness of the Idea, religion and philosophy standing above it. But art can only express the Idea in its own fashion, on

78

a unique and lower level of clarity than can religion and philosophy. As a mode of 'expression,' art is deeply meaningful. In addition to its freedom it, in its own right, disposes of great knowledge-giving value. If, then, one attributes to Hegel's influence two of the important tenets of Cousin's aesthetics,

> l'art considéré d'une part comme une activité indépendante ayant sa fin en elle-même, d'autre part comme une sorte de religion....[99]

the justification of the second tenet must be seen as very different in the two systems. For Cousin's jump from the independence of art as experience to the value of art as experience is grounded in his own Platonic idealism, mainly in the notion of an 'idea' or 'ideal' accessible to aesthetic experience, rather than in the belief that art really is a kind of religion, expressing the Idea. However, Hegel can have helped Cousin to see – as Kant could not have – that the freedom of beauty from any external concerns does not mean the uselessness of beauty, and that freedom and use are interinvolved here. Thus Hegel says that

> dans cette manière de voir (the theory of art as moral instruction), la forme sensible, qui constitue précisément l'œuvre d'art, n'est plus qu'un accessoire oiseux, une simple enveloppe, une apparence donnée expressément comme telle, un ornement extérieur et superflu... La forme et l'idée ne se pénètrent plus,

and:

> De toute production de l'art d'un caractère pur, on peut dégager une idée morale; mais il faut pour cela une explication, et la morale appartient à celui qui sait la tirer; elle dépend de lui...[100]

Cousin recognizes the futility of making art dependent on conceptual morality, while at the same time holding that art is instinct with its own morality:

> En revendiquant l'indépendance, la dignité propre et la fin particulière de l'art, nous n'entendons pas le séparer de la religion, de la morale, de la patrie...,[101]

and:

> l'art est par lui-même essentiellement moral et religieux; car, à

79

moins de manquer à sa propre loi, à son propre génie, il exprime partout dans ses œuvres la beauté éternelle.[102]

The Idea, for Hegel, is presented by art in various concrete forms which determine, respectively, the different arts. The notion of beauty as a 'concrete Idea' is, as Basch claims, apparent in Plato and Plotinus also. I have seen it in Cousin, and related it to the scale of progressively more spiritual beauties which are to be found ascending from inanimate nature to God in the late Platonism of Shaftesbury. As in Plotinus, that theory holds for the form or expressiveness of all creation. With Hegel, of course, such expression is found only in art, the beauty of which is reborn (*wiedergeboren*) in man's spirit. Nature itself is still 'unform.' Yet there *is* support in Hegel for the frequent statement of Cousin's that

> la fin de l'art est l'expression de la beauté morale à l'aide de la beauté physique.[103]

This is the form which Cousin's doctrine of 'expression' usually takes, as aesthetic cognition is for him essentially moral, thus spiritual; he writes:

> Le beau ne serait que le vrai et le bien, s'il n'avait des formes: encore une fois, c'est la forme sensible du vrai et du bien qui les fait devenir ce que nous appelons la beauté. Le beau a donc pour ainsi dire deux parties: une partie morale et une partie sensible. La partie morale, c'est le bien et le vrai, dont le beau est la manifestation; la partie sensible, c'est la forme, sous laquelle le vrai et le bien se manifestent à nos organes.[104]

He assigns the faculty for sense-experience to the sensible part of the beautiful object, and 'raison' to the moral part, which is to be disengaged from the unity within the variety of the beautiful object. Thus Cousin turns the 'concrete Idea,' as it appears in beauty, into the context of a 'beau-idéal'-'beau-réel' relation, in which the two elements are easily separable.

However, in the light of Cousin's Hegelian division of the arts, which like Hegel's is based on this notion of 'expression,' it is possible to doubt the influence of Hegel on Cousin's theory. It should be limited to an influence of form, as it contributes to Cousin's aesthetic only an affirmation of the Platonic doctrine of the spirituality of beauty-experience.

The criterion employed by Cousin for his hierarchy of arts is their degree of moral expressiveness. This quality, he finds, is unattainable unless the particular art is free. Thus he excludes rhetoric, history, and philosophy, as they are all concerned with some kind of utility. Among the arts proper, he gives the lowest rank to architecture and gardening, as they have the least tractable mediums. Hegel, too, not only excludes 'useful' arts, but sees architecture as the art in which the medium (or form) most nearly surpasses the Idea (or content). It is on the basis of the kind of adjustment of content to form that Hegel classifies the other arts, at the same time locating them chronologically. Architecture is a symbolic art, peculiar to early religious thought which struggled to express its sublime Idea, but succeeded only in suggesting it. Sculpture is the classical art, par excellence, in which the Idea is the human form, and is thus perfectly adjusted to its medium. In the Romantic arts, painting, music and poetry, the content becomes progressively less material, and the form less able to express its content. Music is the most subjective and emotional art, while poetry is the most spiritual, the ultimate art, because in it the 'symbols' are no longer ends in themselves, as they are in music, but simply 'stand for' mental images, the words in themselves having become transparent. Poetry, Hegel concludes, foretells the death of art, as in it the Idea has reached fullest aesthetic self-consciousness, and must await further developments in religion and philosophy. Though Cousin constructs no such historical frame for his hierarchy, he does, using his 'expressionist' criterion with the likeness and unlikeness to Hegel's 'concrete Idea,' which I have shown above, reach similar evaluations and even descriptions. Above architecture in terms of freedom of spiritual expression, Cousin finds music the most profound and moving art, while sculpture is as precise and determined as music is vague:

> La sculpture.... ne fait guère rêver, car elle représente nettement telle chose et non pas telle autre. La musique ne peint pas, elle touche; elle met en mouvement l'imagination, non celle qui reproduit des images mais celle qui fait battre le coeur....[105]

Painting, which is

> plus pathétique que la sculpture, plus claire que la musique.... s'élève, selon nous, au-dessus de toutes deux, parce qu'elle exprime davantage la beauté sous toutes ses formes, l'âme humaine dans toute sa richesse et la variété de ses sentiments.[106]

Poetry, though, expresses all that each of the lower arts does, and in addition 'pensée,' which is only partially accessible in each other art. Every idea which poetry renders is at once 'profonde' and 'déterminée,' close both to its sensible and moral aspects. To a degree, then, poetry involves a fusion of its form and content, but only because its form, speaking in Hegel's terms, is threatening to exceed the concreteness of art altogether. Cousin does not, of course, prophesy the death of art, which he believes able to reach the 'idées absolues' as well as are religion and philosophy; but his 'expression' hierarchy, though declining on occasion to a mere description of the emotion proper to each art, is based on a grasp of the sensible-intelligible complex of each art, and so points toward Hegel's classification.

# VI

Perhaps the most obvious feature of this argument still needing to be justified is the disproportionate attention given to expounding the three representatives of the Platonic tradition. I claimed that Cousin is more naturally a Platonic idealist than he is anything else. I implied that that tradition is so native to him that he sees subsequent aesthetic in its light. But he also makes certain compromises with pure Platonism, and the clearest illustration of them can be made by a proof of his misuse of Plato or of his tradition. I discussed Cousin's doctrine of 'ideal beauty,' which posits an abstraction; that doctrine was a distortion of Plato's idea of 'cognitive desire,' and of Plotinus' spiritual monism. Thus Plato's argument that the experience of beauty may attain an Idea of Beauty is changed to an argument that each aesthetic experience contains a 'real' and an 'ideal' element. Likewise, the spiritual bond of artist to nature, which Plotinus justifies by his monism, will by Cousin be maintained alongside the rationalized 'belle nature' of neoclassicism which affords no intellectual idea in its bare state. Cousin was so basically indebted to Plato and Plotinus that these compromises with them must be originally explained in their terms. His misunderstandings of the Platonic tradition are central to his understandings of the two subsequent aesthetic traditions.

What I am describing, then, is a dilution of the pure Platonic tradition, but hardly an important abandonment of it. It might then be asked whether Cousin's aesthetic is full of inconsistencies. It seems to be. But, in the first place, Cousin seldom states contradictory views. Certainly, he does uphold both a 'belle nature' and a nature which is eloquent in its unrationalized 'reality.' Or he will support contradictory attitudes, at one time treating the 'ideal' as a clarified, intellectual statement of reality, at another time as a make-believe world, where all is diffused with a certain magic. More commonly, though, his compromises resemble that by which the Idea of Beauty is confused with the 'beau idéal.' The element common to both notions is that aesthetic experience is spiritual, and so more than just perceptual experience. In fact, each notion holds that the 'terme' of the experience it describes is God, or an Idea emanating from him. It is not hard for Cousin, then, to harmonize the 'esprits' which dominate the two theories. The same fact is strikingly illustrated in his doctrine of 'expression.' I have said that that doctrine is rooted in the Platonic conception, recurring in Plotinus, Shaftesbury, Reid.... of a scale of ascending beauties in nature, which rises through spiritual beauty to God. In each material beauty, the matter is simply an envelope through which inner spiritual beauty expresses itself. Cousin applies this doctrine widely throughout his aesthetic; to, for example, the neo-classicism of Winckelmann or the idealism of Hegel. In the first case, Cousin admires Winckelmann's description of the moral expressiveness in the beauty of Greek sculpture. But Winckelmann, with the neoclassic belief that the 'ideal' reveals itself chiefly in the human body, and with a non-rational conception of 'ideal beauty,' approaches the Apollo Belvedere with preconceptions quite different from Cousin's. From Hegel's 'concrete Idea,' Cousin plainly takes some support for his theory of the ideal-real complex in a beautiful object. And the binding of this doctrine to a hierarchy of arts clearly shows the debt of Cousin to Hegel in this matter. Still, as I have pointed out, Cousin's 'concrete ideal' differs vastly from Hegel's 'concrete

Idea.' What Cousin often does, then, is to take over the aspects of these later aesthetic which he can harmonize with his basic Platonism. The facileness of eclecticism is evident in these compromises. But Cousin cannot be denied a certain grandeur of breadth, for which he pays heavily in depth.

I ask, finally, in what sense it is fair to call Cousin a Platonist in his aesthetic. Even in Roman thought, Platonism had been seriously vulgarized. The chief sources for the Roman view of the platonic aesthetic, in Cicero's *Orator*, and Seneca's *Epistle LXV*, have already both materialized the Idea of Beauty, and abandoned the close attention to 'cognitive desire' which is found in the *Symposium* and even in the *Phaedrus*. The passage from the *Orator* is canonical for the 18th century, and for the neoclassicism which Cousin inherits. But through Plotinus and Shaftesbury, Cousin inherits a more authentic Platonism, though it is in no sense a model of the original. Cousin, therefore, is a Platonist in the permissible senses both of deriving his thought from the master and of deriving it from a wealth of varying progeny of the master. And in a metaphorical sense, as Victor Basch would agree, Cousin could be called a Platonist even when he borrows from German idealism, since that aesthetic tradition is ultimately close to the aesthetic of Platonism.

# Notes

[1] Cited by Bréhier, *Histoire de la Philosophie*, Paris, 1932, vol. II, fascicule III, p. 659.

[2] Cousin, Program of 1818, 'Sur les Vérités Absolues,' in *Fragments Philosophiques*, Paris, 1833, p. 266.

[3] Cousin, *Du Vrai, Du Beau, et Du Bien*, Paris, 1853, p. 169. I will abbreviate this title as *VBB*.

[4] The other, minor writings or statements on aesthetic by Cousin are to be found in the following places: *Archives de 1818*, p. 8; *Cours de 1820* (on Kant), p. 65; *Cours de 1819* second semester, (3e édition, 1857), p. 64 ff., 414; *Fragments et Souvenirs*, p. 84; *Cours de 1829*, 1st volume, in *Hist. de la Phil. du 18e siecle*, (4e édition, 1861), p. 20; 'Du Beau et de l'Art,' *RDM*, vol. 14, 1845, pp. 775 ff.
The last mentioned item is the most extensive writing by Cousin on aesthetic except *VBB*. It is, however, almost exclusively a restatement of ideas expressed in *Du Beau*. The other items are without exception incidental, and need no comment here.

[5] This is essentially what Cousin accuses Diderot of, though he admits that Diderot made many penetrating observations. In the opening of the section *Du Beau* of 1853, Cousin has little admiration for previous aesthetic thought. He points out that the sensualist schools have produced hardly a page on beauty, and that even such distinguished theorists as Kant and Reid have not solved the basic problem of just how the creative artist makes the beauty in things into artistic beauty.

[6] Cousin, *VBB*, 1836, p. 293.

[7] *Ibid.*, p. 254.

[8] *Ibid.*, pp. 259-260.

[9] Cousin, *VBB*, 1853, p. 175.

[10] *Ibid.*, p. 265.

[11] Cousin, 'Du Beau Réel et du Beau Idéal,' in *Premiers Essais de Philosophie*, Paris, 1862, pp. 324-37, for full study of the abstraction involved. Cf. also the following passage:

En même temps que nous admirons les beautés réelles que nous présente la nature, ne nous élevons-nous pas à l'idée d'une beauté supérieure, que Platon appelle excellemment l'Idée du beau...? (*VBB*, 1853, p. 141).

[12] Cousin, *VBB*, 1853, p. 144. Cf. also this passage:

ôtez le sentiment, tout reste froid et inanimé; qu'il se manifeste, tout prend de la chaleur, et de la vie.

[13] Cf. the strongly moralistic avant- propos to Cousin's 1853 edition of *VBB*. We can measure some of the distance between Cousin and the second romantic generation, Flaubert or Baudelaire, by contrasting their views of the way in which art improves over nature. One might say that, for Cousin, art improves nature, while for the 'art-pour-art' thinkers art is an improved nature. It is noteworthy, relative to Cousin's view, that he makes no mention of Aristotle's *Poetics* here, where it could have been so instructive for him, and where it was a standard model for critical theory.

[14] Cousin, *VBB*, 1853, p. 206. There is, as I shall show later, a reminiscence here of Burke's treatment of 'la puissance mystérieuse des mots,' as Cousin calls it.

This passage, with countless others, brings to mind a study which could be made of the relation of Cousin's 'course of thought' to the manner in which he expresses himself. We could follow the method used by Leo Spitzer, in *Linguistics and Literary History*, by showing Cousin's basic mentality in a cumulative, gradated 'souffle' which expresses idealistic 'sentiments.'

[15] Cousin, *VBB*, 1853, p. 154.

[16] Janet, *Victor Cousin et son Oeuvre*, Paris, 1885. Janet respects Cousin highly for his virtual reintroduction of Platonism into France, and proves in detail the dearth of idealistic philosophy at the outset of the 19th century in France.

[17] Bosanquet, *History of Aesthetic*, New York, 1904, p. 29. I disagree with the implication made elsewhere by Bosanquet in his *History*, where he maintains that Plato never conceived beauty as symbolical of spiritual reality. There is an exception in the notion of 'beautiful harmony,' which I shall discuss below.

[18] Bosanquet, *ibid.*, p. 30, writes of the one true aesthetic principle recognized by Hellenic antiquity in general. This may be described as the principle that beauty consists in the imaginative or sensuous expression of unity in variety.

[19] Cf. Plotinus' thought, as rendered by Cousin, that 'les hommes beaux sont seuls juges de la beauté.' The same idea will recur in English criticism, in Sidney and Shelley.

[20] Quoted by Bosanquet, *op. cit.*, p. 33.

[21] Cf. *Laws* (796-802) for the precise prescription given by Plato for the place of musical experience in the state. The relation of mode to the peculiar effect of music is a matter of great concern to Plato.

[22] Plato, *Republic*, 401 D.

[23] Pater, *Plato and Platonism*, New York, 1901, p. 242. To this book, and to a discussion in the *Argument of Plato* by F. H. Anderson, I owe the largest debt for a grasp of Plato's idea of musical culture and of 'cognitive desire.' The implied spiritual monism which underlies Pater's thought, and his own preciosity, make him sensitive to Plato's eductional belief in growth through beauty. Pater believes the child to be unconsciously mimetic of all the beautiful (especially 'repeated') forms which he develops in the midst of. Cf. *Marius the Epicurean* for a profound illustration of this view.

[24] Plato, *Republic*, 206 A.

[25] Cousin, *Cours de l'Hist. de la Philosophie Moderne*, Paris, 1847, p. 178.

[26] *Ibid.*, pp. 175-176.

[27] Cousin, 'Du Beau Réel et du Beau Idéal,' p. 336.

[28] Cousin, *Frag. Phil.*, p. 339.

[29] Cousin, *VBB*, 1853, p. 146.

[30] Plotinus, *Ennead* 5, 8. Bosanquet's treatment of Plotinus' aesthetic, as of Plato's, seems the most searching. By restricting the subjects of his *History* to relatively few thinkers, Bosanquet is enabled to point out their interrelations in detail. Thus the discussion of Plotinus sees him in the context of previous Greek aesthetic thought, Aristotle's as well as Plato's, and strongly establishes his transitional importance.

[31] Plotinus, *Ennead*, 5, 8.

[32] Q. de Quincy, *An Essay on the Nature, the End, and the Means of Imitation in the Fine Arts*, trans. by J. C. Kent, London, 1837, p. 215. The only readily available copy of the work is this unfortunate translation.

[33] *Ibid.*, p. 216. Fuller treatment of the matter must await the second section of this chapter. The typically neoclassical position of Quincy is, however, immediately obvious.

[34] *Ibid.*, p. 277. A translation from a passage in Cicero's *Orator*.

[35] Quotes by Quincy, *ibid.*, p. 275. A careful history of the ideal Zeus of Phidias would be a fine index to changing critical views. This interpretation by Cicero was canonical in antiquity, and was held more or less similarly in major 18th century criticism.

88

[36] Cousin, *VBB*, 1836, p. 300.

[37] Plotinus, *Ennead*, 1, 6. The same adjustment of intelligibles is held by Aquinas, as we have seen it be by Plato.

[38] Cousin, *VBB*, 1836, p. 274. Cf. also *VBB*, 1853, p. 167. Cousin's pantheism was, of course, a much disputed topic between 1830-50, provoking a rash of vituperative anti-Cousin pamphlets as well as the disapproval of such distinguished thinkers as Gioberti and Rosmini. Though it is hard to disengage the sources of that pantheism, there seems to have been a distinct influence from Hegel.

[39] Cousin, *VBB*, 1836, p. 272.

[40] *Ibid.*, p. 273. Cousin refuses to animals the power to judge beauty, a proof that just being beautiful is not sufficient to guarantee the power of aesthetic judgment.

[41] *Ibid.*

[42] Plotinus, *Ennead*, 5, 8. Plotinus is specifically attacking the Stoic theory, which made a proportionate adjustment of material parts the criterion of beauty. Cicero, *Tusculan Disputations*, 4, 13, expounds the Stoic theory.

[43] Plotinus, *Ennead*, 5, 8.

[44] Cousin, *VBB*, 1853, p. 169.

[45] Cousin, *VBB*, 1836, p. 272.

[46] *Ibid.*

[47] *Ibid.*

[48] Ravaisson, *Rapport sur la Philosophie en France au 19e Siècle*, Paris, 1868. Ravaisson's broad-minded treatment of the spiritualist movement, and his location of it in its historical 'cadre,' have never been surpassed.

[49] Cited by Rand, edition of Shaftesbury's *Second Characters*, xxxvii.

[50] The reason why some people want to perfect nature is never taken up in the Platonic tradition, as far as I know.

[51] The tradition in which Cousin's genius- theory falls is distinct from the *ingenium*-tradition, which, in the 18th century, as in Batteux, would imply an ability to copy nature in accordance with rules of decorum. The notion of the genius as distinct in kind from the normal person becomes prominent in the eighteenth century, and is treated complexly by Diderot. It is this notion which Shaftesbury and Kant examine in their different ways. Cf., for a searching treatment of the matter, Dieckmann, 'Diderot's Conception of Genius,' *JHI*, 1941, Vol. II, pp. 151-183.

[52] Cousin, *VBB*, 1836, p. 267.

[53] Quoted by Sternberg, *Shaftesburys Aesthetik*, Breslau, 1915.

[54] Shaftesbury, *Moralists*, Part. 3, Section 2.

[55] Cousin, *VBB*, 1836, p. 254.

[56] Cousin, *Frag. Phil.*, 1833, p. 339.

[57] Cousin, *VBB*, 1853, p. 146.

[58] For the whole tendency of eighteenth century aesthetic toward isolating and defining aesthetic experience, and for careful substantiation of this matter, see Folkierski, *Entre le Classicisme et le Romantisme*, Paris, 1925.

[59] This notion had a great vogue throughout 18th century neoclassical criticism, as Folkierski shows. For the most part, it is exasperatingly nonaesthetic: in Hutcheson the greatest attention is given to the degree of variety which can still be reduced to agreeable unity. A typical statement of the problem is that of Crousaz:

> La variété plaît donc essentiellement à l'esprit humain, c'est un principe d'expérience; il est fait pour la variété, elle l'anime et l'empêche de tomber dans l'ennui, et dans la langueur. Mais il lui faut aussi de l'uniformité au milieu de la diversité... Quoted by Folkierski, p. 70.

[60] Reid, *Essays on the Intellectual Powers of Man*, 1785, p. 458.

[61] *Ibid.*, p. 473.

[62] Quoted by Mackensie, *Critical Responsiveness*, Berkeley, 1949. Mackensie's study of English psychological literary theory in the 18th century is of great use for the student of the faculty psychologies as they were introduced into literary theory.

[63] Quoted by H. M. Dewey, in his thesis on *Herder's Relation to the Aesthetic Theory of his Time*, Chicago, 1920, p. 26. This thesis, incidentally, offers a convenient survey of the major eighteenth century aesthetic theories, though, as the relation of Herder to those theories is shown only after the survey, it inevitably remains external.

The Burkean notion of the feeling of delight in the presence of beauty 'represents' a whole realm of thought toward the close of the eighteenth century. In Diderot, for instance, aesthetic 'enthusiasm' is important:

> L'enthousiasme est un mouvement violent de l'âme, par lequel nous sommes transportés au milieu des objets que nous avons à représenter... Quoted by Margaret Gilman, 'The Poet According to Diderot,' *Romanic Review*, 1946, pp. 37-54. That article presents a good survey of Diderot's anti-classical aesthetic theories.

[64] Cousin, *VBB*, 1836, pp. 250-51.

[65] *Ibid.*, pp. 280-81. It is worth commenting on Cousin's own predilection for using single words effectively. No doubt from the habit of oral expression, he evolved a style with an extremely small vocabulary, but which used periodic phrases so as to bring abstract nouns into high

relief. The relief is the more striking as Cousin almost never employs imagery.

66 For the general historical problem of Platonism in the critical theory of the eighteenth century, see the article by Bredvold, 'The Tendency toward Platonism in Neoclassical Aesthetics,' *ELH*, 1934, vol. I, pp. 99-119. In brief discussions of le Père André, Winckelmann, and Reynolds, he brings out some of the fortunes of 'ideal beauty' in the eighteenth century. There is a discussion of the chief Roman sources of eighteenth century aesthetic, Cicero and Seneca, but perhaps too little emphasis on the difference of Plato from this tradition. That distinction serves more than historical accuracy; it enables one to see more clearly the inconsistencies of neoclassical theory. For an objection to Bredvold's description of Reynolds as a Platonist, see Trowbridge's article, 'Platonism and Sir Joshua Reynolds,' *ES*, 1939, pp. 1-7 . Trowbridge holds that Reynolds was closer to Locke than to Platonism, and was generally hostile to any transcendental Idea of Beauty. The fact is that Reynolds shifted his position on this matter, and reflected the inconsistencies of the pseudo-Platonism of the eighteenth century. If that Platonism is carefully defined, though, there can be no danger in ascribing much of Reynolds' thought to a non-empirical aesthetic. Perhaps best treatment of what Platonism and Neoclassicism are, in the abstract, is Paul Goodman's article, 'Neoclassicism, Platonism, Romanticism', *Journal of Philosophy*, xxxi, 1934, pp. 148-63.

67 R. D. Havens, 'Simplicity, A Changing Concept,' *JHI*, vol. xiv, 1953, pp. 3-32. This article presents a finely documented survey of the variations in the understanding of 'simplicity' as a concept, especially during the Augustan and Greek Revival periods.

68 Quoted by Croce, *Aesthetic*, London, 1922, p. 263.

69 Bosanquet, *op. cit.*, p. 250.

70 Quoted by R. D. Havens, *op. cit.*, p. 26.

71 For the problem of the 'characteristic' in aesthetic, see especially Bosanquet, *op. cit.*, pp. 311, ff. The introduction of this concept marks one phase in the breakdown of the neoclassical aesthetic. Its formal introduction was made by Goethe's friends Hirt and Meyer. Meyer believed that the principle of ancient art was the 'significant,' and that its successful treatment resulted in the 'beautiful.' For Hirt, the 'characteristic' was 'the intention of nature as expressed in generic or specific characters.' Hirt's view is far from the naturalistic one which the word 'characteristic' connotes today, but still demands the expression of a 'natural' perfection. Goethe's major attempt to solve the 'characteristic'-'ideal' opposition can be found in his dialogue *Der Sammler*

*und die Seinigen* (1798). There he suggests that it is 'beauty' which gives life to the scientific expression of the 'generic,' and 'softens the significant and lofty,' the ideal qualities of the work. This attempt to preserve the useful connotations of the 'ideal' was short-lived, but indicated the most practical continuation of Winckelmann's position.

[72] René Schneider, in his *L'Esthétique Classique chez Q. de Quincy*, Paris, 1910, shows what a revolution in Quincy's conception of antiquity was brought about by Elgin's transportation of the Parthenon 'marbles' to England in 1812; a series of such revelations of Greek art marked the first fifteen years of the 19th century. Schneider can say, in describing Quincy's doctrine:

> C'est celle de Winckelmann, amendée et complétée par les révélations d'Égine, de Phigalie, du Parthénon, et de l'île de Milo. Dès 1816, l'historien et l'esthéticien germano-italien ne suffisait plus à personne, surtout en France; de fait et de volonté, Quincy est le Winckelmann français... p. iii.

It is hard to see how Winckelmann was able to evoke his 'ideal' theory from the late and relatively 'naturalistic' works of sculpture which were available to him. But just as Lessing, who found a quiet grandeur in the Laokoon, Winckelmann was doubtless moved by a feeling of the sudden (though not profound) quality of 'suspension of time' which works of Hellenistic sculpture so often seem to express.

[73] In his essay on Winckelmann, in *The Renaissance*, Pater quotes a famous judgment by Hegel: "Winckelmann, by contemplation of the ideal works of the ancients, received a sort of inspiration, through which he opened a new sense for the study of art. He is to be regarded as one of those who, in the sphere of art, have known how to initiate a new organ for the human spirit."

[74] Cousin, *VBB*, 1853, p. 165.

[75] Q. de Quincy, *De l'Idéal*, 1837, p. 46.

[76] For the wealth of difficulties awaiting any theory of 'ideal beauty' see the treatment by Saisset, in his 'examen critique' of French aesthetics, which follows his *L'Ame et la Vie*, Paris, 1864, pp. 91-167. In his clear-sighted criticism, Saisset shows the confusion between the multiplicity and unity of the Idea of Beauty, and expounds the difficulties involved in determining whether each individual, each 'type,' or each 'genus' has its peculiar 'ideal.'

[77] Quoted by Garrett, 'The Imitation of the Ideal,' *PMLA*, 1947, pp. 735-44. This non-beautiful ideal is related to the 'characteristic,' which, in Hirt for example, meant simply the natural generic perfection proper to any being. At the point, not yet reached by Quincy, at which all traces of a transcendent Idea of Beauty have been forsaken, the

92

neoclassical aesthetic shades gradually into a form of 'naturalism,' though a highly rationalized one.

[78] In 1801, the Institut had proposed as subject for its essay contest: "Quelles sont les causes de la perfection de la sculpture antique et quels seraient les moyens de l'atteindre?" Quincy lost this contest to Eméric David, who, in his essays published in 1805 as *Recherches sur l'Art Statuaire*, had argued that the best Greek sculptors had directly copied nature.

[79] Quoted by Garrett, *op. cit.*, p. 741.

[80] Cousin, *VBB*, 1853, p. 177.

[81] *Ibid.*, p. 179.

[82] Cousin, 'Du Beau et de l'Art,' *RDM*, vol. 14, 1845, p. 775. This article by Cousin on beauty is virtually an abstract from his sections on beauty in *VBB*.

With regard to Lessing's taste for the pale and pure, it should be remembered that he deplored the invention of oil painting. Like Mengs, for example, he believed that the truest beauty was the purest beauty. Cf. Meng's Platonic affirmation:

> All Nature is beautiful, and so is virtue; beautiful are forms and proportions; beautiful are appearances and beautiful the causes thereof; more beautiful is reason, most beautiful of all is the great first cause. Quoted by Croce, *op. cit.*, p. 226.

[83] Cousin, *ibid.*, p. 781.

[84] Cousin, *VBB*, 1853, p. 183.

[85] Victor Basch, *op. cit.*, p. 364.

[86] This would seem to be true, despite Hegel's view that art is an inferior form of philosophy, a less clear stage of the Geist in its progress toward self-consciousness. That view hardly lowers the evaluation of art in Hegel's thinking, as it is expressed in the *Philosophie der Kunst*. In no writer is a profounder sympathy with the unique value of aesthetic experience evident. Cf. for a good summary of Hegel's aesthetic, Stace, *The Philosophy of Hegel*, London, 1934.

[87] Cousin, *VBB*, 1836, p. 231.

[88] Cousin, *ibid.*, p. 224.

[89] *Ibid.*, p. 224. This passage has become famous as a *locus classicus* for the statement of the doctrine of 'l'art pour l'art.'

[90] Cousin, *VBB*, 1853, p. 140.

[91] Cousin, *ibid.*

[92] Cousin, *ibid.*, p. 141.

[93] Cousin, *VBB*, 1836, p. 231.

[94] Cousin, *VBB*, 1836, p. 248.

[95] Cousin, *ibid.*, p. 247.

[96] Cousin, *ibid.*, p. 267.

[97] Cf. Knoop, *Victor Cousin, Hegel, und Die französische Romantik*, 1932, p. 93.

[98] Quoted by Knoop, p. 93.

[99] Paul Stapfer, *Questions Esthétiques et Religieuses*, Paris, 1906, p. 51. Stapfer considers those two tenets 'les principes essentiels du grand professeur français' (Cousin), and is content to see Cousin's aesthetic as stemming chiefly from Hegel. Despite an overemphasis on the German influence in Restoration France, Stapfer brings out the serious personal contribution of Cousin to French aesthetic.

[100] Quoted by Stapfer, p. 51.

[101] Quoted by Stapfer, p. 49.

[102] Quoted by Stapfer, p. 50.

[103] Quoted by Knoop, *op. cit.*, p. 92.

[104] Cousin, *VBB*, 1836, p. 284.

[105] Cousin, *VBB*, 1872, p. 200.

[106] Cousin, *ibid.*, p. 203.

94

# Index

96